KU-170-459

Seán Swayne

Gather Around the Lord

A vision for the renewal of the Sunday Eucharist

the columba press

the columba press
8 Lower Kilmacud Road, Blackrock, Co. Dublin, Ireland.

First edition 1987
Designed by Bill Bolger
Typesetting by Typeform Ltd, Dublin
Printed in Ireland by
Mount Salus Press, Dublin.

ISBN 0 948183 48 9

Copyright ©, 1987, Seán Swayne

GATHER AROUND THE LORD

Contents

For
Paddy McGoldrick

Abbreviations

Conciliar and post conciliar documents:

SC	*Sacrosanctum concilium,* Vatican II, 4 December 1963
IGMR	*Institutio generalis Missalis Romani,* 6 April 1969
MS	*Musicam sacram,* 5 March 1967
LI	*Liturgiae instaurationes,* 5 September 1970
DVD	*De verbi Dei,* 21 January 1981
MC	*Marialis cultus,* 2 February 1974
EM	*Eucharisticum mysterium,* 25 May 1967
IGHL	*Institutio generalis de Liturgia Horarum,* 11 April 1971
LG	*Lumen gentium,* Vatican II, 21 November 1964

Abbreviations referring to books of the bible follow those of the Jerusalem Bible.

Introduction

I am happy to have the opportunity of making available these reflections on the Sunday Eucharist.

Fourteen years ago I was asked by the Irish Bishops to work for the renewal of the liturgy as secretary to their Commission for Liturgy.

That work has been for me a privilege.

I have had opportunities, not afforded to others busily involved in the pastoral scene, to ponder deeply the mystery of the holy Eucharist, and to share my reflections over the years with innumerable audiences from young adults to senior clergy.

My transfer recently back to parish work seemed an appropriate time to write up some of these reflections, together with points of particular interest from publications not accessible to the average reader, and make them available at a wider level.

Gather Around the Lord is the result.

I offer it in the hope that others, when they gather round the Lord at Sunday Eucharist, will do so with an even greater degree of understanding, commitment and love.

That too is my prayer.

I am dedicating the work to a close friend, Father Paddy McGoldrick, priest of the diocese of Derry, and professor of liturgy at Maynooth.

Few, if any, have worked so hard, so consistently and so effectively for liturgical reform in this country, and even beyond the confines of this country, as Paddy McGoldrick. But that work has gone on largely behind the scenes. Meantime I, like so many others working on the more popular front, have been standing on his shoulders. To Paddy I dedicate this book with gratitude and admiration.

Seán Swayne
Graignamanagh
Easter 1987

Sunday Mass, The Christian's Weekly Encounter with The Risen Lord

"Without the Sunday eucharist we cannot go on living" – the martyrs of Abitina, 12 February 304.

It is in the Sunday eucharist that the Christian experiences the Lord's presence most intently and most intimately.

One of the most remarkable accounts of Mass in the early centuries has come down to us from the pen of Augustine. Writing in 426 he describes the opening of a Mass prior to which a miraculous cure had just taken place:

> I advanced towards the people. The church was full. Cries of joy echoed through it: "Glory to God! God be praised!" Nobody was silent. Shouts were coming from everywhere. I greeted the people, and again they began to cry out in their enthusiasm. Finally, when silence was restored, the readings from the sacred scriptures were proclaimed.[1]

True, it was not a normal occasion. And yet one wonders if a somewhat similar picture could not have been drawn for any Mass of that period. Certainly one gets the impression from the writings of the early Fathers that Sunday Mass in those early centuries was a joy-filled, festive celebration. The faithful knew that the Lord was alive. While still on earth he had promised not to abandon them, but to be with them all days even to the end (*Mt 28:2*). And whenever two or three of them would gather in his name he would be there in their midst. The Fathers applied this latter text from Matthew (*18:20*) above all to the gathering together for the eucharist. Gathering for Sunday eucharist was a gathering around the person of the risen

1. Quoted in R. Cabié: *The Church at Prayer,* vol 2, Geoffrey Chapman, London 1986, page 50.

Lord. It was the Christian community's weekly encounter with him, when they could experience his presence most intently and most intimately. Without that weekly experience life had nothing to offer, as the martyrs of Abitina in Tunisia indicated at their trial on 12 February 304: "Without the *dominicum,* the Sunday eucharist, we cannot go on living."[2]

So it was for the early Christians. So it must be once again for us today. Mass is our weekly rendezvous with the risen Lord. Around him we assemble, we who are his own. To his table he invites us, beckoning us to come to him, sinners though we are.

Host at Table

Here it may be necessary to emphasise the distinction between the presence of the Lord on the altar-table and *at* the altar-table.[3] The tendency in popular piety was to focus on the presence of the Lord *on* the altar-table. Indeed in the same popular mind Mass was seen primarily as a means of procuring that presence for purposes of both adoration and communion. However, prior to thinking of the Lord as being on the table as the food which nourishes us we should think of him *at* the table as the host who invites us. And by 'table' we are not thinking of the physical table only but of the entire eucharistic setting or gathering. It is to that gathering that we are summoned: "Come to me", he says. "Come, take, eat, drink. All who are thirsty, come. You who have no money, come. Pay attention. Come. Listen and your soul shall live" *(Mt 11:28; 26:26-7. cf Is 55:1-3).*

And so we go to meet the Lord on the day of the Lord, week after week of our lives. We listen to his word. We join him in praising the Father and in offering the sacrifice. We commune deeply and intimately with him in sacramental communion. And from the entire experience we draw strength to go out from Mass to imbue the world with the spirit of the Gospel.

Real Presence and Real Absence

A question to pose here is: how can the real presence of the Lord be reconciled with his real absence? Since the Ascension Jesus is no longer earthbound, no longer with us in a bodily way. His followers

2. The trial of the 49 Christians, 31 men and 18 women, took place at Carthage.

3. A point made by Father Eugene LaVerdiere at the 11th Annual Carlow Liturgy Seminar, 1982.

saw him with their eyes, looked upon him, touched him *(1 Jn 1:2)*, but that cannot be our experience of him. His bodily presence has been withdrawn from us. And yet although we are deprived of his bodily presence we are not deprived of his real presence.[4] For in the celebration of the eucharist he is present to us just as he was present to his contemporaries, except that we cannot see him. He is present to us in just as real a manner, guiding us, reassuring us, gathering us up into his eternal self-offering to the Father. This is what was foretold in Matthew 28:20 where "the all-powerful Son of Man promises his dynamic, energising, enabling presence to his pilgrim Church as it moves ever farther into space and time."[5]

All this is by the power of the Spirit. Indeed the risen Lord through the power of the Spirit is present to us in an even more effective way than he was to the disciples.[6] He is present in a way which makes it possible for every Christian of every generation to come into immediate personal contact with him. And the privileged moment of that contact is the celebration of the eucharist.

So, as Augustine says: "He has ascended without leaving us. While in heaven he is also with us, and while on earth we are also with him."[7]

The real absence, therefore, which accompanies the real presence is an absence which points to a future when we shall see him face to face. To that future we look forward with the ancient Christian prayer on our lips: "Maranatha! Come, Lord Jesus!" *(1 Co 16:22)*.

New Testament Insights

Two incidents in the New Testament give an insight into the realness of the Lord's presence as experienced in their eucharists by the first generation of Christians. One is in John's Gospel, chapter 20, an account of the first post-resurrection assembly of the disciples. It is the evening of the first Easter Sunday. The disciples are assembled behind locked doors in a room in Jerusalem. Suddenly Jesus is

4. See R. Taft in *Worship,* January 1981.

5. John P. Meier, *Matthew,* Veritas Publications, Dublin, 1984, page 373.

6. "Once he had returned to the glory of his Father's majesty, in a mysterious way he began to be more present to his disciples in his godhead, once he had become more distant in his humanity" – *Pope St Leo the Great, Sermon 2 on Ascension, 1-4.*

7. Sermon on Ascension, *The Divine Office,* vol 2, page 627, Collins Dwyer Talbot 1974.

standing in their midst, calming his frightened followers with his greeting of peace (*Jn 20:19*). Here we have a glimmer, however faint, of what the first generation of Christians must have experienced when they assembled for their eucharist on the day of the Lord. Into their assembly, even though visible only to the eyes of faith, came their Lord, risen, alive, glorious.

The other incident is that of Emmaus. Here again the account is coloured doubtlessly by the writer's experience of the eucharist of his own day with its "explanation of the Scriptures" *(cf Lk 24:32)* and "breaking of bread" *(v 35)*. At any rate, when all is over we find the two disciples recalling: "Were not our hearts burning within us as he spoke to us on the way" *(v 32)*. Such was their reaction. Such too must have been the reaction of the first generation of Christians to the presence of the Lord in their eucharists.

From these two incidents we would like to conclude that the early Christians had a vivid and intense awareness of the real presence of the Lord in their Sunday assemblies. At those assemblies "their eyes were opened" (*Lk 24:31*), their hearts "burned within them" (*Lk 24:32*), they recognised him "in the breaking of the bread" (*Lk 24:35*), they acclaimed him as their Lord and their God (*Jn 20:28*).

And so we assemble Sunday after Sunday, not in order to placate God or to fulfil a legalistic obligation but to encounter in a real and intimately personal way the living Lord. And the spirit of the occasion is festive. It is a spirit which rises above the moods and emotions of the individuals who make up the assembly. Some may be there in a spirit of elation, others in a mood of near depression. Some may bring to the eucharist feelings of well-being and success, others feelings of failure and brokenness. It matters not. The eucharist is always festive, because it is always a celebration of what God has done for us in Christ, always a breaking in upon the self-offering which the Son is eternally making to his Father in heaven. The eucharist calls therefore for song and celebration, for music and ceremonial, for lights, vestments and incense. For the Lord around whom we assemble, the Lord 'at the table', is the Lord who has conquered death and sin, and who will empower us in turn to conquer death and sin, failure and brokenness.

Recovering a Sense of Presence

The practical question remains. How can we in our day recover something of that vivid awareness of the presence of Christ which characterised the eucharists of the early Christians? Here we recall four modes of Christ's presence which have been receiving attention in recent years: his presence in the faithful, his presence in the word, his presence in the priest, and his presence *speciali modo* in the sacred species. Each presence, according to the Church's magisterium, is a *real* presence *(EM 9)*.

With regard to the Lord's presence in the word, already that presence is spelled out quite clearly in the ritual of the Mass (for instance through the reverence shown to the book of the Gospels), in preaching and catechesis. Furthermore it can be said that an awareness of this presence has penetrated deeply into the sensibilities of Catholics since the Vatican Council. Nor would there appear to be any pastoral problem with regard to the Lord's presence in the sacred species, an awareness of which, and a focussing upon which, has characterised christian worship over the centuries. The problem arises in relation to the other modes of Christ's presence – in the people and in the priest.

A priest presiding at the eucharist does so not so much *in place of Christ* but *in the person of Christ* (*in persona Christi*). This statement conveys the age-old belief of Christians that it is Christ who acts at Mass. It is Christ who reaches out to the faithful through the humanity of the priest, through his words, his gestures. It is Christ who, 'masked' by the priest (the Latin word 'persona' means mask), presides over them, leading them in prayer to the Father. And he does so through the priest. In this sense the priest at Mass *is* Christ, sacramentally.

How can all this be evoked ritually? First, by signs of reverence to the person of the priest, standing as he enters the assembly, standing again as he leaves at the end. The honour of course is to Christ. For this reason it is better, as someone has pointed out, for a commentator at the entrance procession to invite the faithful to "stand and greet the Lord with song" rather than to "stand and greet the priest with song." Again, people's awareness of the presence of Christ in the priest can be heightened by having a worthy place of presidency, marked by the 'chair of Christ', which is the focal point of attention at the beginning of the celebration. For the same reason attention ought to be paid to the vestments the priest wears, the manner in which he enters the assembly, the incensation of the priest. All are expressions of the Church's belief that Christ is present in the person of the presiding priest at Mass, leading us in the worship of the Father.[8]

Finally there is the question of the presence, and again we emphasise that it is a real presence, of Christ in the people. Someone has said that it is easy to recognise Christ in the sacred species, but less easy to recognise him in the people.[9] How then can people recover an awareness of his presence? Preaching and catechesis will help. But here we are concerned rather with spelling out the Lord's presence in the people through signs, reinforcing it through the ritual of the celebration.

First of all it will be necessary to ensure that the tabernacle is located outside the area of the attention of the people during Mass; otherwise the focussing may tend to be on the Lord's presence in the reserved Sacrament. In this connection it is interesting to note that in the *Caeremoniale Episcoporum* of 1982 it is laid down that when the bishop is on his way to preside at Mass, he and the ministers do not stop to reverence the reserved Sacrament if they must pass by it on the way to the sanctuary.

The places of the faithful are another important factor. They should be such that the people are seen to be a gathered people, relating to one another in a warm, human way.

The opening rites should be used to help focus the people's attention on the Lord's presence in their midst. Occasionally the opening song could make specific reference to that presence. And the priest's greeting is seen by the missal itself as expressing the presence of the Lord in the assembled community (*IGMR 28*).

If occasionally the incensation of the people is carried out during Mass, the minister should incense them with the same reverence with which he would incense the Lord in the blessed Sacrament.

An awareness of the presence of the Lord among them will bring peace and joy to the celebrating community, a peace and joy which will dispel any temptation to that disunity which is incompatible

8. It has been argued that less attention should be paid to the entry of the priest in order to allow for a focussing on the Lord's presence in the people. The argument is scarcely convincing. Both modes of presence can be emphasised.

9. Towards the end of the film *The Mission* the soldiers make the Sign of the Cross when they come into the presence of Christ in the Blessed Sacrament procession. They then proceed to massacre that same Christ in the Catholic Indians.

with eucharist, and which sunders the body of Christ.

On the other hand, that awareness will stay with the people as they go out from their assembly, and will inspire them to see the Lord in one another, in the poor, the needy, the suffering, and the 'little ones' of daily encounter.

On the morning of the first Easter Sunday the young man at the tomb who told the women that Jesus had risen added: "Tell his disciples and Peter that he will go before you into Galilee. There you will see him" *(Mk 16:7)*. Our Galilee, the Christian's Galilee, is the eucharistic assembly. To that Galilee we hasten on the day of the Lord. There we will see him.

The Sunday Assembly

"The only error they admit to is their custom of assembling on a certain day before dawn to sing hymns to Chrestos as to a god" – Pliny, 112.

One of the most pressing pastoral challenges in relation to Sunday Mass is to liberate people from their individualism, and bond them into a eucharistic community.

One day while on a visit to Rome I called in to San Clemente as Mass was being celebrated. It was a week day, and the congregation was small. The language was Italian, the texts and chants unfamiliar, the people all strangers to me. I felt I did not belong – until the sign of peace. It was then I experienced an intense feeling of belonging. These were my people, my own people, the people of God, the 'assembly'. I felt at home.

Notwithstanding the Second Vatican Council's stress upon the communal nature of christian worship (eg *SC 6, 10, 26, 41, 42, 106; LG 11, 26)* many Catholics continue to have a rather individualistic approach to the celebration of the Sunday eucharist. For them religion is a matter between the individual and God, and when it comes to any kind of involvement through, for instance, singing or taking part in a function or ministry, they prefer to be left alone.

However, Christianity is not a matter between the individual and God, but between the individual *and the Church* and God. It is through the Church, the community, that salvation comes to the believer. The Church is the body of Christ. It is the People of God. And it is above all in that Church that one can come into contact with the word of God, receive God's healing and forgiveness, and become personally involved in the offering of Christ's sacrifice. Here then is one of the most pressing pastoral problems of today in relation to Sunday eucharist: to liberate people from their individualism; to help them see themselves not as so many individuals, journeying through life in splendid isolation from one another, but as a people, bonded together in the Lord.

Sense of Church among Early Christians

The early Christians had a deep sense of 'church'. They saw themselves as *a people* with a common belief in the Lord, a common commitment to him, a common sharing in his life, a common concern for his kingdom. Their law was the law of love, their mission the proclamation of the Gospel, their goal the kingdom. From the beginning, therefore, they organised themselves to worship as a people. For it was when they assembled to worship that they were most conscious of themselves as a people. It was this practice of assembling for worship that was to become the distinguishing feature of the Christians' way of life, even for pagans like Pliny, quoted at the head of this chapter. "In the eyes of the historian", according to A.G. Martimort, "assembly is the first and most basic liturgical reality."[1]

The Middle Ages saw the erosion of this sense of assembly and its replacement by a spirit of individualism. One factor which helped bring about the change was the development of the 'private' Mass and the gradual estrangement of the people from the liturgy. Masses in which congregations sang and joined in acclamations and prayers, and in which different lay ministers carried out different functions such as reading and chanting, were replaced by Masses in which only the voice of priest and server were heard, and where the priest carried out the functions of the lay ministers as well as his own. So it was to remain more or less until the eve of Vatican II when Sunday Mass was still seen as something one attended in order to fulfil a precept rather than as the Christian's weekly encounter with the risen Lord in word and sacrament, and in the company of the baptised.

1. I wish to acknowledge help received from various articles by the person to whom credit must go for reviving an awareness of the liturgical assembly in our day, Monsignor A. G. Martimort. See *The Church at Prayer*, vol 1, Irish University Press, 1968, article on 'Assembly', revised in the new edition of *L'Église en Prière*, Desclée, 1984 currently being translated; his articles in *La Maison Dieu, 20, 40, 57* and *60*. Also Joseph Lécuyer: the 'Liturgical Assembly, Biblical and Patristic Foundations' in *Concilium 1966*. J. Stephen O'Brien (ed): *Gathering God's People*, National Catholic Education Association, 1982. A masterly treatment of the subject will be found in *Roles in the Liturgical Assembly*, 23rd Liturgical Conference of Saint Serge, Pueblo Publishing Company, New York, 1981.

Recovering our Sense of Church

To return to our initial question: how can our Sunday congregations recover that sense of 'church' which characterised early Christian worship? In this connection it will be helpful to re-read closely the early chapters of the Acts of the Apostles. The picture which emerges of the life and worship of the first generation of believers is nothing less than inspiring. First we note, perhaps surprisingly, that these Christians continued to worship in the synagogue and temple. At the same time they were initiating a new practice which was to become the distinctive feature of their way of life. This was the practice of *assembling* to worship as a people.

References to the Christian assembly in *Acts* are many. Immediately after the Ascension, for example, the followers of Jesus *assemble* for worship in an upper room in Jerusalem (*Ac 1:12 f*). It is as they are *assembled* on the day of Pentecost that the Spirit comes upon them *(Ac 2:1)*. The author adds a detail here, which also occurs in *1:15; 2:44:* he tells us they are assembled *epi to auto,* a phrase which conveys the idea of being one in heart and mind – something not evident in the usual translation 'in one place'. During Peter's imprisonment we find the Christians *assembled* at prayer in the home of Mary, mother of John Mark (*Ac 12:12*). At Antioch the *assembly* is gathered by Paul and Barnabas (*Ac 14:27*). Finally, at Troas, the author tells us "we were *assembled* on the first day of the week to break bread" (*Ac 20:7*).

The importance of the assembly comes out still more vividly when we turn to Paul and to *Hebrews.* For Paul the assembly is Christ himself. To offend against it is to offend against the body of Christ, as is clear from *1 Corinthians.* Moreover, in order to maintain a spirit of love and unity in the assembly each member must be prepared to put aside his or her own concerns for the sake of the good of the whole body. *Hebrews* is concerned about people who at this stage are beginning to stay away from the assembly; for the author, Christians gathered at the assembly are one with the angels in festal gathering, and one with the just who have already gone to be enrolled in heaven (*Heb 12:22-24*).

Finally, we turn to the early Christian writers outside the New Testament, where we find some remarkable references to the Christian assembly. The author of the first century *Didaché* says to the readers: "On the day of the Lord *assemble* to break bread and to offer thanks . . ." (*ch 14*). Some years later, around 150, Justin tells how "on the day called after the sun, all from towns and country *assemble*" for the eucharist.[2] Ignatius of Antioch, around 105, is concerned like the author of *Hebrews* about those people who neglect to come to the assembly. In the century following, the author of the *Didascalia Apostolorum* reminds the same absentees that they are "sundering and scattering the body of Christ" (*ch 13*).

However, for the most beautiful development of the catechesis of assembly we must wait for the writings of John Chrysostom in the fourth century. Stressing the power of communal prayer, and the importance of the faithful appreciating the power of communal prayer, he says: "If Jesus is in the midst of two or three people gathered together, with all the more reason is he present where such a large body of men and women are present."[3] Again he writes: "Do not say; 'What! Can I not pray at home?' Of course you can. But your prayer has more power when it is joined to that of other members, when the whole body of the Church lifts its prayer up to heaven with a single heart."[4] And a final text: "Let us therefore close up together. Let us bind one another together in love. Let no one separate us."[5]

So, we arrive at our picture of the life and worship of the early Christians. It is that of a people with a strong sense of identity. They are the new People of God, in continuity with the *Qehal Yahweh* or people whom God bonded together at Sinai (*Ex 19*). They are what Peter called "a chosen race, a royal priesthood, a holy nation, God's own people" *(1 P 2:9-10)*. Through acceptance of Jesus and baptism they have become members of that people, the body of Christ, called by God in the Spirit *(LG 26)* and "linked together by Christ with the chains of love".[6] It is above all when they assemble to worship that they give expression to that fact that they are a people, and are most clearly seen as a people. It is when they assemble, too, that they can experience in the most intense way possible the presence of their

2. *First Apology, 67.*

3. *On Genesis, 6, 1.*

4. *Homily on Obscurity of Prophets, 2, 4.*

5. *Homily on 2 Thess, 4, 4.*

6. *Commentary of St Cyril of Alexandria on Letter to the Romans,* quoted in *Divine Office,* vol 2, page 577.

Lord, risen, alive and glorious. And so they assemble. Frequently. And the spirit of their assemblies is one of prayer and praise, unity and togetherness, joy and festivity. So it was in the beginning. So it must become, once again, in our day.

The Christian Assembly

The Second Vatican Council emphasised, as has already been mentioned, the communal nature of Christian liturgy. In at least three places the *Liturgy Constitution* speaks of the faithful "coming together" for the eucharist, and not just participating in it. (*SC 6, 10, 106*). And the Missal itself reflects this same sense of togetherness: "In the Mass . . . the people of God are *called together* to celebrate the memorial of the Lord . . . " (*IGMR 7*). Today as a result, a sense of assembly is beginning to come back into the christian consciousness, although participation *as assembly* seems to be seen more in terms of the faithful's association with the presiding priest (responding to his greetings, praying with him, actively attending to what he is doing and saying on our behalf) than in terms of their relationship to one another. Two further points must be made, therefore, if this sense of assembly is to be developed: the first concerns ritual expression of assembly-awareness; the second, the taking seriously of reconciliation as a pre-requisite of assembly.

1. Ritual expression of Assembly-awareness

Unlike any other assembly, e.g. at a football game, the liturgical assembly is already a community, even if this is not perceived by people. Those who are present, even if unknown to one another, are related through their common faith and love and sharing in the life of Christ. Their common calling cuts across barriers of race, colour, age, language. But, people are human, and their awareness of themselves as a people needs to be heightened through human visible expression. In particular this awareness needs to be ritualised, especially at moments such as the opening rites, the sign of peace, the communion.

The opening song is an important bonding moment. Its purpose, in addition to opening the celebration, introducing the people to the feast or mystery being celebrated, and accompanying the procession, is "to deepen the unity of the people" (*IGMR 25*). Blending of voices makes for blending of hearts, a blending to be lived out in daily life.

Through the celebration of the liturgy in song "the unity of hearts is more profoundly achieved" (*MS 5)*.

Communion time is another moment which can express and strengthen the sense of unity. Moving towards the table of the Lord in orderly procession, and joining our voices in song as we go along, can be a powerful ritual expression of the "spiritual union of all communicants" (*IGMR 56*). A well arranged procession conveys the joy-filled festive spirit of the assembly, and alerts people to an awareness of the ties which bond them together in the Lord.

Prior to all this is the physical setting for the assembly. Serried rows of benches, in which the faithful are regimented, fastened up in their own individualism, lacking freedom of movement and gazing at the backs of heads in front of them, are not conducive to a sense of gathering and assembly. Seating arrangements should be such that they facilitate the active participation of the faithful, their freedom of movement and their opportunity to relate to one another in a warm human way. The people we are accommodating are the community of believers, one in heart and mind, gathered together in the Lord, and taking a full active part in the liturgy (*cf Ac 4:32, IGMR 7*).

Added to this is the manner in which people relate to one another as they enter the church and await the celebration. They must cultivate within themselves a welcoming heart, a heart which even when weighed with human grief radiates the peace and joy of the Lord. This spirit of welcome and graciousness will permeate the whole celebration, and will find expression in the care with which one shares a hymn book, passes a collection plate, or facilitates those coming and going past at communion time.

Finally there is the human extension of assembly-awareness which finds expression in our sensitiveness towards people outside Mass. This can be fostered, for example, by offering a cup of coffee after the celebration in an adjacent hall or even at the back of the church. And so our awareness of others extends into the sanctuary of the world.

2. Reconciliation

Of all the horrible reports emanating from the troubles in Northern Ireland the worst was the incident in which three men on their way to an 'execution' – one of them being the condemned man himself, the others being the 'executioners' – first went to Mass. If one needs proof of the existence of the demoniac, there it is in that blasphemous travesty of the liturgy.

A pre-requisite for liturgy is reconciliation. Jesus said so in the celebrated text in *Matthew* about offering one's gift, after having first been reconciled *(5:23)*. Matthew's text reflects also, no doubt, the awareness among Christians of his day that they dare not approach God in liturgy without first being reconciled. To be unreconciled with another is to be unreconciled with God. If we do not forgive, neither will God. The first century writing, the *Didaché*, makes a similar point: "On the day of the Lord, assemble. Break bread and offer eucharist . . . Anyone who has a difference with a neighbour is not to assemble with you unless they are first reconciled. Otherwise your sacrifice will be profaned" *(ch 14)*. In the *Didascalia Apostolorum* of the third century we read: "Anyone who is contentious or makes himself an enemy to his neighbour diminishes the people of God . . . If you hold any malice against another, or another against you, your prayer is not heard nor your eucharist accepted." The same author records how the deacon, in those times, as Mass is about to begin, announces in a loud voice "Is there any person here who has something against another?" And if there is, the presiding bishop has a word with them, and gets them to make it up, apparently on the spot! Many such citations could be added to show how seriously our early Christian forebears, notwithstanding their own lapses (as, for example, in the feuds which broke out in Paul's time in Corinth and which flared up again a generation later according to the first Epistle of Clement), took the Lord's command to forgive and to be reconciled, especially before attempting to celebrate the liturgy.

To reconcile people, to unite and gather them, this is an essential part of the mission of the people of God. Today, once again, the assembly must concern itself with that unity of hearts of which the early church was the supreme model. And the assembly must begin with itself, so that it will become a sign and a reminder to the world of how the Lord is gathering together into one all his children who have been scattered *(Jr 23:3; Ezk 34:11f; Jn 11:52)* through sin and disbelief.

Reverence at Mass

"Reverence is the secret of all religion and happiness. Without reverence there is no faith, or hope or love" – Canon Sheehan in *Luke Delmege*.

An attitude of awe and reverence should permeate the entire celebration of the eucharist.

The celebrated Columba Marmion, prior of Mont César from 1899 and abbot of Maredsous from 1909, left behind him a reputation for joviality, geniality and warmth. Monks who remembered him used say how they always knew when he had visitors from his native Ireland because of the gales of laughter emanating from the monastery parlour. One incident Marmion often recalled, with amusement, happened on the occasion of a visit to his home country. A neighbouring widow had a sick cow, and sent for the holy Benedictine to bless it. Marmion went across to the farm and blessed the cow. The cow expired immediately! During the celebration of the liturgy, however, the same Don Columba seemed to be a transformed person. Incidents which would send a ripple of laughter through the choir stalls, such as a snore announcing that a member of the community had nodded off into a sleep, left Dom Columba unaffected. He had crossed the threshold into another world, the world of the transcendent.

Absence of Reverence

An absence of a sense of awe and reverence, and an increasing loss of the sense of the sacred, has been a characteristic of much liturgical celebration in the post-conciliar era. By 'reverence' we are not of course thinking of some kind of mystification or obscurantism, but of the kind of atmosphere which serves to remind us that in the liturgy we are caught up in communion with the God who is the God of glory and majesty as well as being our Abba, Father.

In this connection we may recall Paul VI's concern about "the attitude of those who try to drain liturgical worship of its sacred character", or of Paul Tillich's warning against "covering up the experience of the sacred under the dust of daily living".[1] True, nothing is definitively profane in the redeemed world – sin alone excepted. At the same time because we are human we have a need for what someone has called "the sacred oasis in the midst of the secular" to remind us that everything is sacred. Yves Congar refers to the 'sacred' as "the domain of realities (things, words, persons etc) through which we experience the divine"; and he adds: "the sacred quality of a space, a building, a painting, a piece of music, stems from its capacity to 'compose' us and place us in a state favourable to prayer."[2] In this way the "pedagogical sacred", to use Congar's own expression, can facilitate us in finding the Lord in the liturgy.

Here we look at some areas where problems relevant to our discussion sometimes arise:

Music. Much has been achieved in this field. Beautiful compositions in the vernacular are appearing, and tribute must be paid to the countless people throughout the church who are spending themselves in the promotion of church music. On the other hand one can only shudder at the distress still being caused by the mawkish, trite and uninspiring music still being inflicted on so many Catholic congregations, music which stays far from "raising the mind to heavenly things" *(MS 5)*.

The vernacular. The introduction of the vernacular has been a blessing indeed, but not an unmixed blessing. 'Banality' is a word frequently heard from the older generations whose ears were accustomed to the grandeur of the Latin. However, we must not be harsh with the people who worked day and night in the aftermath of the Council to meet with our impatient demands for an instant vernacular translation, a translation which we were glad at the time to welcome. Hopefully standards will improve as the excellent work of current revision programmes proceeds.

The artistic environment. Liturgy calls for a climate of awe, mystery and wonder. Poorly designed furnishings, shoddy vestments, tawdry

1. From a conference given by Paul Tillich at the National Conference on Church Architecture, USA, shortly before his death.
2. 'Situation du "Sacré" en régime chrétien' in *La Liturgie après Vatican II,* Les Éditions du Cerf, 1967.

altar appointments and tasteless decor militate against such a climate and in fact incur the disapproval of our Church authorities (*SC 124*). An environment lacking in beauty is "an environment basically unfriendly to mystery and awe, an environment too casual, if not too careless, for the liturgical actions."[3] The gaudy, the vulgar, the cheap and the inauthentic have no place in Christian worship.

One may recall in this connection Paul VI's memorable discourse to artists on 7 May 1964 in which he said "We ask your pardon. We have abandoned you. We have treated you in a worse manner. We have had recourse to substitutes, to oleography, to inexpensive works of art of little merit. We have taken byroads along which art and beauty and, what is worse for us, the worship of God has been badly served."

The use of ritual. Another feature of many liturgical celebrations today is the stripping away of their emotive appeal from the sacred rites, and the reducing of liturgical communication to the level of the verbal and the conceptual. Many will recall the celebrated article of Annibale Bugnini in 1975, when the famed promoter of the Council's liturgical renewal programme took to task those priests who were adopting a minimalist approach to the celebration of the eucharist, and ignoring the opportunities offered by the *pro opportunitate* clauses in the Missal which allowed for the solemnisation of the liturgy whenever appropriate. Bugnini appealed for the restoration and fuller use of symbol and ritual, the neglect of which was leaving the liturgy impoverished. He called for the generous use of incense in festive celebrations, the more careful use of candles, the development of processions at Mass, the restoration of good taste and neatness in vesture, the discreet use of flowers. "To strip the sacred rites of so much of their emotive appeal is to impoverish them, to reduce them to a skeleton shrivelled and shrunk."[4] Liturgy is emotion, Romano Guardini used say, but emotion under strictest control.

The presiding priest. Too often the presider's handling of the liturgy betrays that chummy approach to God which is in marked contrast with the sense of awe which all through the centuries has been a characteristic of Christian worship. One St Patrick's Day eucharist,

3. *Environment and Art,* USA Bishops.

4. *New Liturgy,* No 7, page 17.

not in my own country, opened with the song 'It's a great day for the Irish', with the 'Legend of the Emerald Isle' in place of the first scripture reading, and the response 'Too-ra-loo-ra-loo-ral etc' during the psalm. And there was worse. Doubtless the planners of the celebration meant well. Perhaps they were trying to wed the sacred to the secular, or to bring the human celebration into the sacralising sphere of the liturgy. But the effort was desperately misguided, and if that is creativity then, as the old Irish priest said, it would be better "keep to the tarred road".

In liturgy as in the priestly ministry generally the priest is the servant of the faithful, and the servant of the Church's worship. Within the parameters of the Roman Missal the priest can and ought to be creative, adapting the format of celebration to the particular assembly, availing of the various options which are at his disposal, and in general trying to give spirit to the letter of text and rite. Tampering is of a different order. The faithful have a right to authentic worship, worship which they know has the Church's seal of approval. To deprive them of this right in the name of creativity can be tantamount to 'falsification', to use a rather strong term from St Thomas Aquinas,[5] and can leave the faithful pained and bewildered. "The priest should realise that by imposing his own personal restoration of the sacred rites he is offending the rights of the faithful and introducing individualism and idiosyncrasy into celebrations which belong to the whole Church" (*LI*). Informality, yes, as Pope Paul VI used to say, casualness, never.

If the faithful are to experience a sense of awe and wonderment during the celebration of the sacred mysteries, the presiding priest himself must first be seized with an awareness of the presence and proximity of the God of glory and majesty. *Cor ad cor loquitur.* Heart speaks to the heart. "This comes from the heart", Beethoven wrote on the score of his Missa Solemnis, "may it speak to the heart." A reverent approach on the part of the priest – in word, gesture, posture, action and attitude – will in turn project itself onto the experience of the congregation. What comes from his heart will speak to their hearts.

The other ministers. Much of what has already been said about the priest will apply to the other ministers, all of whom should be aware of the dignity of their ministry and the responsibilities which accom-

5. *Summa Theologiae,* 2-2, Q. 93, a. 1.

pany it. The readers' concern for their ministry will be reflected for example not only in the care with which they prepare and proclaim the scriptures, but in the very manner in which they carry the book, walk to the ambo, and announce "This is the word of the Lord." Psalmists will aim not only at singing prayerfully and beautifully, but at trying to foster an atmosphere of prayer, and to hold the congregation in prayerful reflection after the proclamation of the word. Readers of the intentions at the prayer of the faithful will strive not only to read clearly and audibly, but to facilitate the faithful as they exercise their priestly duty of praying for the world; in other words the readers here will try to make this a real moment of prayer for the faithful. Eucharist ministers will distribute the body of the Lord with a reverence which will be infectious; in giving Communion they are creating communion. And so on with all the ministers. Prayerful, serious preparation of their ministry will contribute powerfully towards building up in the church the kind of atmosphere in which people will more easily move into the world of sacred mysteries.

Our Concept of God

In the context of all this discussion a review of our notion of God can be of value.[6] All too often, the point is frequently made, we try to bring God down to our own human level. We adopt a casual, matey approach which is scarcely conducive to that sense of wonderment one would expect from the believer in the presence of the Creator. A glance back into the Old Testament can help restore that image of God which has characterised Jewish and Christian liturgy over the centuries, the image of God as the *rex tremendae maiestatis,* the king of indescribable majesty. In the presence of this God the attitude of the believer has always been one of awe and reverence and wonderment.

So, for example, when Ezekiel glimpsed the glory of the Lord his reaction was to fall upon his face in awe *(Ezk 1:28)*. Daniel fell prostrate during his vision *(Dn 8:17)*. And Moses at the burning bush hid his face "for he was afraid to look at God" *(Ex 3:6)*. The attitude of the believer in the presence of God is captured nowhere more beautifully perhaps than in the psalms: "O Lord, O Lord, how majestic is your name in all the earth . . . When I see the heavens, the

6. I find Verheul: *Introduction to the Liturgy,* Anthony Clarke Books, 1969, page 22 most helpful here.

work of your hands . . . what are we that you should keep us in mind?" (*Ps 8*). "The Lord is king; the peoples tremble" (*Ps 98*). "O give the Lord, you children of God, give the Lord glory and power" (*Ps 28*).

Nor does this image of God belong to the Old Testament only, in spite of the over-simplification one sometimes hears that the God of the Old Testament is the God of forbidding transcendence, whereas the God of the New is the God of inviting nearness. One thinks, for example, of Peter prostrate at Jesus' knees, following the miraculous catch of fish, crying out "Depart from me, O Lord, for I am a sinful man" (*Lk 5:8*). Or the three visionaries prostrate before Jesus on the mount of transfiguration *(Mt 17:6)*. Or the disciples 'dumbfounded', when Jesus calmed the storm and the lake, wondering "what sort of man is this that even the winds and the sea obey him?" *(Mt 8:27)*.

Here then we see the normal reaction of the believer when he or she comes face to face with God in worship. It is a reaction which grips one's whole being, and which finds expression naturally in external acts of gesture, posture, manner of speaking and general ritual movement. Only when we have bent our hearts in awe before the God of the cosmos will we be able to appreciate the intimacy with which God loves us in such a deeply personal one-to-one relationship, with all the care and tenderness of a mother *(Is 49:15)* and all the concern and protectiveness of a Father *(Mt 6:26)*.

The same awe which has characterised the attitude of the believer in the presence of the Lord, whether in Old Testament or in New Testament times, has likewise characterised the celebration of the Christian liturgy over the centuries. This is so above all in the Eastern rite churches where an atmosphere of mystery and the sacred is facilitated through the splendour and magnificence of the ritual, and "where men and women, according to their capacity and desire, are caught up into the adoring worship of the redeemed cosmos; where dogmas are no barren abstractions but hymns of exulting praise."[7]

But not only in the East. At the beginning of the eucharist in the Mass of the Roman Rite we are reminded that what we are preparing to celebrate are "the sacred mysteries". The God of our eucharistic worship is the "God of all creation", the "God of power and might", the "God of glory and majesty", the God whose glory we proclaim,

7. Hammond: *Waters of Marah,* 16, quoted by Robert Taft in *Beyond East and West,* The Pastoral Press, Washington, DC, 1984.

together with angels and saints, in words borrowed from the bible's account of the vision of Isaiah: "Holy, holy, holy!" God is also the "holy God", the "fount of all holiness", "living in unapproachable light", the God of "splendour", the "God of glory and majesty". In the presence of this God one attitude alone is valid: that of reverence and love, awe and wonderment. Anything less ill befits the celebration of the sacred mysteries.

The Mass and Social Justice

"God does not need golden vessels but golden hearts" – St John Chrysostom.

There is an essential connection between Mass-going and our duties in justice towards those in need.

An English Catholic newspaper once carried a little child's drawing of the Mass with the caption: "The Eucharist is about caring."[1] The following week a correspondent protested, criticising the child's teachers for the inadequacy of their teaching on the Eucharist.

The child was right. The eucharist *is* about caring. It is about many things – sacrifice, memorial, banquet, presence and so on.[2] But it is also about caring or, as John the Evangelist would have put it, about foot-washing – serving others "to the end" (*Jn 13:1*), to the point of laying down one's life for one's friends (*Jn 15:13*). It is to such service that Christians commit themselves, by the blood of Christ, when they go to Sunday Mass.

Mass and Social Justice, the essential Link

Sunday Mass ought to be an incitement[3] to the faithful to concern themselves about the needy in their midst. This claim is based on the essential connection between the eucharist and social justice, an awareness of which has been mounting especially since 1981 when the great International Eucharistic Congress on the theme 'Jesus Christ, Bread broken for a New World' took place in Lourdes.[4]

1. The *Universe,* 26 September 1986.
2. See p 45.
3. I borrow the word 'incitement' from the *Les Dombes* statement of 1972 which says "The celebration of the eucharist is . . . an incitement not to accept conditions in which people are deprived of bread, justice and peace."
4. The whole inspiration for this article is owed to Father Dermot Lane for his remarkable paper at the Congress, a paper which "deserves much more attention than it has had so far" according to Owen F. Cummings in the *Clergy Review* of June 1986. Father Lane's paper will be found in the collection *Eucharist for a New World,* Irish Institute of Pastoral Liturgy, 1981. Thanks is also due to Owen F. Cummins for the article referred to, which readers will find challenging.

Failure to link liturgy with life is not a new phenomenon. Eight centuries before Christ the prophet Amos railed against worshippers whose lives lacked justice and integrity "Thus says the Lord: 'I hate and despise your feasts, I take no pleasure in your solemn assemblies . . . Take away from me the noise of your songs; to the melody of your harps I will not listen. But let justice flow like water, and integrity like an unfailing stream' " *(Am 5:21-24)*. We find the same condemnation of worthless worship in Sirach (*34:18-22*) and in Isaiah: "Bring me your worthless offerings no more, the smoke of them fills me with disgust . . . I cannot endure festival and solemnity. Cease to do evil, learn to do good, search for justice, help the oppressed" *(1:13, 17)*. What the prophets were condemning was not the Jewish liturgy in itself, but the hypocrisy of the well-to-do who thought they could honey over their own maltreatment of the poor, and calm their consciences by financing elaborate, pompous ceremonial.

Turning to the pages of the New Testament we find Paul berating those Corinthians who celebrated the eucharist in an attitude of selfish indifference to the 'have-nots' in the community *(1 Co 11:20f)*. The concern of the Apostle James about social justice is perhaps less frequently adverted to. In his Epistle he attacks class distinction among Christians, and reproaches them for neglecting the poor members in the liturgical assembly (*2:2-4*).

The Fathers, too, point up the link between eucharist and social justice. The very first description of the eucharist outside the New Testament, from Justin Martyr, *circa* 150, refers to the collection which was taken up among the better off worshippers for the benefit of the widows and orphans in the community. And so concerned is the author of the *Didascalia Apostolorum,* written early in the third century, about poor people present at the eucharist, that he tells the bishop to give his seat to the poor old person who has no seat, even if the bishop himself has to sit on the ground. We take a final citation from John Chrysostom: "Do not honour Christ here in church clothed in silk vestments, and then pass him by unclothed and frozen outside . . . God does not need golden vessels but golden hearts" (*Hom 50, 3-4*).

The human heart does not change, and Sunday congregations in our own day include many people who would appear to see little connection between going to Mass, on the one hand, and that concern for the poor which ought to characterise the life of the Christian, on the other. For such people Sunday Mass continues to be a privatised matter with no social implications. The result is a scandal. And the first to be scandalised are the youth, who, once they find in the lives of their elders no evidence of any relationship between Mass-going and social justice, tend to write off Mass-going as irrelevant. The problem, therefore, and the challenge is to authenticate in our living what we celebrate in our ritual.

The Foot-washing Incident

Here we turn for light on our discussion to the foot-washing incident in John's Gospel, chapter 13. The essentials of the story are familiar. During the last Supper on the eve of his death Jesus gets up from table and proceeds to wash the feet of the disciples. It was an unforgettable gesture which showed, among other things, that discipleship involves loving others as Jesus did; loving them "to the end" (*Jn 13:1*), that is, utterly and completely; and being prepared to prove that love by our self-giving and humble service of one another. So it was for the first disciples. So it must be, once again for us. To be a Christian is to be prepared to spend oneself in the service of others, and to do so no matter what the cost. In Jesus' case the cost was the cross. In our case the cost is also the cross, the cross of daily effort towards those in need.

Modern commentators hold that John's omission of the institution narrative in his account of the last Supper, and its replacement by the foot-washing incident, was a deliberate attempt to bring home to us the connection between the two: both reveal the meaning of Jesus' death in terms of self-giving and service of others to the ultimate degree. In other words, the eucharist, like the foot-washing, implies commitment to the service of others, commitment to being broken like Jesus for the sake of a better world. Or, to look at it yet another way: the Christ who is present in the eucharist is the same Christ who is present in the poor. One cannot choose to love Christ in the eucharist and scorn him in the poor. Commitment to Christ in the eucharist is commitment to Christ in the poor.

A Practical Question

The practical question remains: if commitment to social justice is knit into the very fabric[5] of eucharistic worship, can a format of celebration of the eucharist be found which will sensitise worshippers to this commitment, challenge them, disturb them? In striving towards such a format it should be kept in mind that a precondition will be a proper mentality on the part of the presiding priest. The presider who is sensitive in this respect will have the effect, inevitably, of alerting his weekly congregation to the social implications of their Mass-going. In particular, his attitude will colour his handling of the following 'moments' of the celebration:

i. *Penitential rite.* While this rite is concerned with praising God and imploring his mercy *(IGMR 29-30)* it can be handled occasionally in such a way as to raise the consciousness of the congregation to an awareness of their responsibilities to the needy in their midst.

ii. *The Homily.* Again, the homilist's concern for the redressing of social ills will filter through his preaching.

iii. *The Prayer of the Faithful.* Occasionally intentions can be included which will have reference to the poor, the deprived, those suffering from injustice. Praying for such people – and the point can be made in the very formulation of the intentions – implies a readiness to work towards the alleviation of their problems.

iv. *The Collection.* So often the collection appears as an unwelcome intrusion into the Mass. In fact if properly handled it can be a powerful weekly reminder of our duty in charity towards our brothers and sisters in need. Our donation then becomes an earnest of our willingness to share with the needy – to share not just the money which we may not have, but our time and our love.

v. *Sign of Peace.* This is a gesture of intent to live in love, to put into practice in the course of each day the love of others to which we recommit ourselves in the eucharist.

vi. *Rite of Dismissal.* This is the moment of mission. In the final 'monitio' which he is allowed to speak at this point the priest could occasionally refer to the mission and challenge which awaits the con-

5. I borrow the expression from Cummins, *op cit:* "Commitment to social justice is not an optional extra for a Christian, but is knit into the very fabric of his eucharistic worship", page 211.

gregation as they take their leave. With God's blessing upon them the people go out now to celebrate the liturgy of the world. Their task is to carry the Christian message to others, to make of their lives a living sacrifice of service, and to go on breaking bread with the needy in the sanctuary of the world.[6]

6. Father Edward Schillebeeckx makes the point in his *God is New Each Moment,* T. & T. Clarke, Ltd, Edinburgh, 1983, that while the contemplative element is indispensable in liturgy, liturgy without social commitment becomes reduced to mere sentimentality; and social commitment without prayer often becomes "grim and barbaric", page 124.

Mass, an Experience of God

"These celebrations of the sacred mysteries must be an experience of prayer" – Pope John Paul II at Edinburgh, 31 May 1982.

If Mass is to be experienced as an experience of God, the priest must alert people to the voice of the Lord coming through the scripture readings; he must create within them a hunger for the word; he must form them in attentive listening, he must help them ponder the word; finally, he must lead them to respond to the word in the offering of the sacrifice, and in the way they live.

I once heard two teenagers say in a radio programme that they no longer went to Sunday Mass. Instead, they had begun to visit their church outside Mass time, and pray alone in quiet silence. Their problem, and it is the problem with many today, is that they are not finding Mass an experience of God, "an experience of prayer". Many Catholics have precisely this problem in mind when they say "we cannot pray at Mass", or "we cannot pray the Mass". A Mass in which God is not experienced is a Mass in which the internal dimension of worship is lacking. It is true, of course, that worship has its external dimension: it seeks expression in word and song, in ritual and ceremonial, in posture and gesture and movement. If the external dimension is lacking worship becomes stultified. On the other hand if worship remains purely external, then it ceases to be worship, and we are left with hollow ceremonial – "sounding brass and tinkling cymbal". Worship therefore must come from the heart. It must be external, but it must also be and "above all" internal (*MS 15*) "ut in primis interior sit opportet".

Herein lies the challenge to all involved in the renewal of the liturgy: to facilitate this internal dimension of worship. It is not enough for the priest, for example, to celebrate the eucharist validly, lawfully and devoutly. He must lead people into and through an experience of God. Not that he is guardian over people's access to God; only God himself can admit people into an experience of himself. But the priest must preside in such a manner that the faithful will more easily experience the celebration as an experience of prayer, an experience of God. People ought to be able to say when the celebration is over: "Yes, we experienced God in this Mass: we heard and took to heart the message of Christ; we joined Christ in praising the Father; we were personally involved in offering the sacrifice; and we experienced intimate communion with Jesus-Eucharist."

Here we look at these four moments of eucharistic worship: listening, praising, offering the sacrifice, and sacramental communion.

I Listening to God's Word

Listening to God's word presupposes that we believe in God's word, that we hunger for it, that we listen attentively to it, that we ponder it and respond to it. If listening is to be effective, then when the liturgy of the word is over we ought to be able to say as the first generation of Christians used say after their eucharist: were not our hearts burning within us as he spoke to us? (*Lk 24:32*).

The first task of the priest in relation to the liturgy of the word is to strengthen people's faith in Christ's presence in the word, to sensitise them to the message which he speaks to them personally and intimately while the scriptures are being proclaimed: "When the scriptures are read in the liturgical assembly Christ himself is speaking to us" *(SC 7)*. The word of God is a contemporary word. As we listen to it we become contemporaries of those people to whom it was originally addressed, two thousand years ago and more. So, we can identify with the various personages who appear in the readings. We are Paul, for example, to whom the Lord is saying: "My grace is enough for you. My power is at its best in weakness." We are those faint-hearted to whom the Lord is saying: "Courage, do not be afraid . . . Look, your God is coming, coming to save you" (examples from readings for 14th, 21st and 23rd Sundays, year B). What was written for them, and spoken to them, was written and spoken also for *our* instruction (*cf Rm 15:4*).

To believe in the word is to acknowledge too the piercing power of the word, which cuts through our indifference, penetrating the very depths of our being. André Louf has gathered together some of the expressions used by the early Christian writers to describe the effect of the word: it *touches* our hearts, it *wounds,* it *needles,* it *pierces,* it *cleaves* open, it *jolts.*[1] The classic example is the Pentecost event where

1. *Teach us to Pray,* Darton, Longman and Todd, 1976, page 38.

God's word "cut (the people) to the heart" (*Ac 2:37*) and they cried out: "What shall we do?" The *Introduction* to the revised Mass *Lectionary* reminds us that all this is brought about through the power of the holy Spirit, whose activity "conveys to the heart of each individual in the assembly of the faithful what is said to all of them" (see *pars 5 and 9*). "The bible possesses sacramental power" writes Kallistos Ware, "transmitting grace to the reader, bringing the reader to a point of meeting and decisive encounter."[2] Our starting point, therefore, in interiorising the word in the liturgy is to have a "lively faith" (*cf DVD 47*) in the piercing power of Christ's message which comes to us in the celebration of the word.

(A beautiful meditation on the power of the word and in particular on the text in Hebrews "The word of God is living and active, sharper than any two-edged sword" will be found in Volume III of *The Divine Office* (Collins Dwyer Talbot, 1974), page 704 in the reading from the works of Baldwin of Canterbury, Office of Readings.)

Hungering for the Word

A second task is to create in the hearts of the faithful a hunger and a yearning for the bread of the word. As the faithful sit to listen to the first reading they could be encouraged to pray with Samuel: "Speak, Lord, your servant is listening"; or with Peter, in the text quoted above: "Lord, to whom shall we go? You alone have the message of eternal life"; or with the psalmist: "Lord, it is your face that I seek. Hide not your face from me."

The Syro-Phoenician woman in seeking access to the table of the Lord longed even for the crumbs. What is offered to us, however, is abundance, "rich fare" (*SC 51*) for the taking, inexhaustible fountains from which to satiate our thirst.[3]

Attentive listening

"If today you hear his voice, harden not your hearts" (*Ps 95*). One wonders how many people at Mass listen, listen attentively, to the word of the scriptures. No doubt the media in our day have weakened people's listening ability. Television advertisers vie with one

2. *The Orthodox Way,* Mowbrays, 1979, page 149.

3. See *The Divine Office,* vol 1, page 518-9. Office of Readings. Commentary of St Ephraem on the Diatessaron.

another and resort to extraordinary measures to capture the attention of viewers. In relation to the word of God, however, dullness of hearing has been a perennial problem, bound up obviously with our sin-permeated condition. The scriptures themselves reproach us for not listening. Isaiah, for example, speaks of people whose ears are open, but who yet do not hear *(42:20)*. Jesus, in turn, makes Isaiah's reproach his own *(eg Mt 13:13f)*. He grieves when people are not open to his message *(Mt 23:37)*. He appeals constantly to people to listen: "He that has ears to hear, let him hear" *(cf Mt 7:26; Lk 9:44)*. He commends those who do listen *(Mt 13:16)*.

I have before me a charming little picture of a monk sitting with hand cupped to his ear, listening to the word of God. It is the attitude which the faithful should have as they sit to listen to the scripture reading at Mass – with hands cupped to ear, so to speak. The same attitude is to be found in the words of Margaret Daly's hymn *Listen to the Word* (adapted from the Rule of St. Benedict):

Open your eyes to the light!
Open your ears to the word!
Today if you hear his voice,
harden not your hearts,
but listen,
listen to the living word of God.[4]

For attentive listening, silence is a precondition; the two are inseparably bound up. Silence creates that space in which the word of God can be listened to without distraction.[5] It is when peaceful silence is "reigning over all" that the all-powerful word comes down among us.[6] Everything 'external' should combine to bring about this atmosphere of 'peaceful silence' – the bearing and pace of priest and reader, the music, the ceremonial, the beauty of book and ambo, the artistic and architectural setting. It is in such an atmosphere that the listening heart is formed.

Pondering

Here our exemplar is Mary: "And Mary kept all these things, pondering them in her heart . . . His mother kept all these things in

4. *Alleluia! Amen! Supplement,* Irish Institute of Pastoral Liturgy, 1981.

5. *cf* André Louf, *La Voie Cistercienne,* Desclée, 1979, page 96.

6. *cf* Entrance Antiphon, 2nd Sunday after Christmas *(Ws 18:14-15)*.

her heart" *(Lk 2:19, 51)*. Speaking on Mary's 'pondering' Pope Paul VI wrote: "The Church also acts in this way, especially in the liturgy, when with faith she listens, accepts, proclaims and venerates the word of God, distributes it to the faithful as the bread of life, and in the light of that word examines the signs of the times and interprets and lives the events of history" *(MC)*.

Pondering the word, then, we look at our lives and at our world, trying by the light of the word to identify our failures, and endeavouring by the strength of the word to realign our lives and our world to the Gospel.

Again, André Louf's gathering together of relevant expressions, this time from the scriptures, helps us to tease out the meaning of 'pondering' God's word: one takes in and digests the word, one cherishes it, harbours it in the heart, clings to it, embraces it, murmurs it day and night *(Ezk 3:1-3; Jb 23:12; Ps 119:11; Lk 8:15; Ac 16:14; Ps 1:2)*.[7]

Pondering the word in this way, the Christian becomes a *tabernacle* of the Lord, as St Jerome says: "Happy will they be who will be the tabernacles of Christ."

Responding

Our response is a two-fold one: first the ritual response; secondly, the active response of daily living out of the Gospel. In the ritual response we greet and proclaim Christ, we praise him for his word: "Thanks be to God! Glory to you, Lord! Praise to you, Lord Jesus Christ." These responses are carried through into the ceremonial, through the ritual postures of sitting and standing, through signing ourselves at the Gospel, through reverencing the book with candles and incense and procession. Our response is ritualised too in song, with the responsorial psalm and the Gospel acclamation.

Secondly there is the active response of Christian living: "When God communicates his word he always expects a response in the form of listening and worship 'in spirit and in truth' *(Jn 4:23)*. The holy Spirit makes the reponse effective, so that what is heard in the liturgical celebration is given expression in our lives, in accordance with the text: 'be doers of the word, not hearer only' *(Jm 1:22)*" *(DVD 6)*.

This commitment to responding actively to God's word, through

7. Louf, *op cit*, page 46.

the living out of the Gospel in daily life, is expressed with effect in words spoken long before the coming of Christ, the words of the Israelites in response to the theophany on Sinai: "All that the Lord has spoken we will do" *(Ex 19:8; 24:3, 7)*.

Here, then, is the challenge to the priest and to all involved in liturgical renewal if the liturgy of the word at Sunday Mass is to become once again a veritable experience of God: to sensitise people to the voice of the Lord coming through the readings, to create within them a hunger for the word, to form them in attentive listening, to help them ponder the word and apply it to their lives, and finally to lead them to respond to the word by the way they live.

And a precondition is that the priest himself be possessed by the word of God.

II Praising the Father

In the first part of the Mass the faithful go through an experience of listening to God. In the second part, the eucharistic prayer, which is the centre and highpoint of the entire celebration *(IGMR 54)*, they go through an experience of praising God and offering sacrifice. Or so they ought to. For the meaning of this prayer is that they "join Christ in acknowledging the works of God and in offering the sacrifice" (*IGMR 54*). Unfortunately people seem to have lost their ability to pray the eucharistic prayer. The old silent Mass had led them to look on it as the priest's prayer, whereas in reality it is the prayer of the whole assembly, though proclaimed on behalf of all by the priest.

And so the question: how can the eucharistic prayer be experienced once again as a prayer of praise?[8] How can it be experienced as a prayer of offering? The answer will involve forming our people into a praise-people, developing among them an awareness of their covenant-commitment, and securing their attention and involvement during the actual proclamation of the eucharistic prayer.

A Praise People

The most basic religious attitude of the People of God is one of 'eucharist', that is, thanksgiving and praise.[9] For this, praise, is our

8. For purposes of the present study we substitute the term "praise" for the phrase "acknowledging works of God".

9. Verheul: *Introduction to the Liturgy*, Anthony Clarke Books, 1968, page 86.

primary response to "the works of God", above all to what he has achieved for us in Christ. Similarly for individual Christians: our basic attitude ought to be one of praise. When we pause to think that all comes from God, there wells up within us a sense of gratitude which flows over in our prayer of praise.[10] The primary motive of our praise is of course the Easter event, our redemption in Christ. So, Augustine could say: "We are an Easter people, and Alleluia is our song." Unfortunately in practice our prayers of praise can be rare, and many will admit that when they pray they are usually petitioning God for a favour, or asking forgiveness for some fault.

Jesus himself is the praise-person par excellence. He came of a praise-people, a people "formed by God to announce his praise" (*Is 43:21*), a people whose songs, the psalms, were charged through with praise. Jesus himself was a true son of these people. The scriptures show him who called (us) out of darkness into his own marvellous light" *(1 P 2:9)*. It is interesting to note that the prayer of praise came easily prayers to be said over bread and wine in his memory – are above all prayers of praise. Of the two actual prayers of Jesus recorded by the synoptics one is, significantly, a prayer of praise – the jubilant outburst in *Mt 11:25:* "Father, Lord of heaven and earth, to you I offer praise . . . "

Like Jesus, like our spiritual ancestors the Jews, we too, Christians, are a praise-people, commissioned at baptism "to sing the praises of him who called (us) out of darkness into his own marvellous light" *(1 P 2:9)*. It is interesting to note that the prayer of praise come easily to our forebears in Ireland. Prayers like "Moladh le Dia", "Praised be God" and "Thanks be to God" were part of the everyday language. And they still are.[11]

Recovering Our Sense of Wonderment

Recovering a spirit of praise means recovering, first, a sense of wonderment. "To praise God is to express our wonderment over the goodness of being alive", writes Dr Ralph Keifer.[12] Father Paul

10. Paul Hinnebusch, OP, *Praise, A Way of Life,* Word of Life, Ann Arbor, 1976. page 1.
11. One traditional Irish song begins: "It's a soft day, thank God."
12. In *To Give Thanks and Praise,* National Association of Pastoral Musicians, Washington DC, 1980, page 143.

Hinnebusch describes praise as "our joyous response to God's glorious self-giving". And he adds: "God created us that we might have joy in loving him, and this joy like all joy overflows in praise."[13] One of the needs of Christians today, therefore, would seem to be to recover their capacity to wonder, to allow their attitudes to be re-charged with a sense of wonderment at the beauty, the power, the majesty of God mirrored in nature, in the cosmos, in the world around us; wonderment too at the transcendent holiness of God. And having recovered our ability to wonder we will find that the prayer of praise will come easily to the forefront of our worship.[14]

All this, the Christian's praise of God, is most powerfully crystallised in the eucharistic prayer. For in the eucharistic prayer our praise is transformed. We can praise God of course in the privacy of our room, or in the midst of our work. But when we bring our praise – for life, health, talents, friends, for a happy marriage, for a new baby – when we bring that praise to the celebration of the Eucharist, our praise becomes transformed, divinised, deified, Christified. It ceases to be *our* praise, and becomes part of the great hymn of praise which the risen Lord is eternally offering to our Father in heaven. Christians "do well always and everywhere" to give God praise. But the privileged moment of praise, the golden moment of praise, is in the sacrifice of praise, the eucharist.

III Offering the Sacrifice

We turn now to the second part of the Missal's statement: "the meaning of the eucharistic prayer is that the faithful join Christ in acknowledging the works of God *and in offering the sacrifice*" (*IGMR 54)* . And we ask: how can God's people actually experience the "offering of the sacrifice" during the eucharistic prayer?

Catholic doctrine on offering the sacrifice at Mass is rich and multifaceted. Moreover, within the parameters of that doctrine each of the faithful will have his or her own favourite viewpoint. One such viewpoint we are going to discuss here. We do so however against the background of the Church's fuller understanding of the

13. *Op cit,* page 1.

14. "At the start of all religion there must be a gazing at God as the source and sum of all goodness and excellence, and the expressing to him of our recognition of his greatness and lovableness" – Cardinal Hume on the Duty to Praise God, *Tablet,* 29 September 1984.

eucharist, which can be fairly summed up in a credal statement such as the following:

I believe that
the Mass is a sacrifice
  in which the sacrifice of the cross
  is made present in our midst
  and perpetuated throughout the ages;

the Mass is a sacred banquet
  which Christians celebrate
  in response to the Lord's words:
  "Do this as a memorial of me";

the Mass is a memorial of the Lord's death and resurrection
  by which the Father through the Spirit sanctifies the world
  and we through the Spirit are reconciled with the Father;

the Mass is a communion
  in the body and blood of the Lord
  really, truly and substantially present
  in the consecrated bread and wine;

the Mass is our at-one-ment with the risen Jesus
  in his relationship with the Father
  in the unity of the Spirit;

the Mass is a foretaste of that heavenly banquet
  to which the blessed are called
  in the kingdom of the Father;

the Mass is a renewal of the new covenant
  in which through the blood of Christ
  we are bonded to the Father
  in a new and fuller relationship;

the Mass is the presence of Christ
  now in the glory of heaven
  yet present too in our midst
  in people and priest
  in word and in sacrament;

the Mass is our 'thank you' to the Father
for all his wonderful works
and especially for the redemption
achieved through his Son;

the Mass is the summit
and the source
of all Christian life;

the Mass is the sign of, and the means of bringing about
through the power of the Spirit,
the gathering together in unity of God's scattered children;

the Mass is the culmination
of the entire worship of the Church
offered to the Father through the Son
in the holy Spirit.

And I believe that

in the Mass the sacrifice which Christ offered
once for all on the cross
is made present and accessible to us
so that we can be personally involved in the same offering;

in the Mass we are united by the Spirit with Christ
in his giving of himself
to the Father;

in the Mass the whole Church offers Christ,
and the whole Church is offered by Christ,
to the Father;

in the Mass the priest offers the sacrifice
in the person of Christ,
and becomes identified sacramentally
with Christ the high Priest;

in the Mass the faithful, who through baptism
share in Christ's priesthood,

join in offering the divine victim to the Father,
and with him, themselves;

in the Mass the power of Christ's cross is applied
for the remission of our failures and sins;
and the entire creation is restored to God
through the paschal mystery of redemption;

in the Mass Christ takes
into his own self-giving to the Father
the spiritual sacrifices which fill our lives as Christians:
our praise and gratitude,
our sorrows and concerns,
our sufferings and our witness;

in the Mass we pledge ourselves
by the blood of Christ
to follow the Christian Way
and to go on breaking bread with the needy
in the sanctuary of daily life;

in the Mass is given to us
a pledge of future glory
when we shall know God as he really is
and see God face to face;

in the Mass we become one with angels and saints,
and one with our loved ones in heaven,
singing with a single voice
a single chorus of praise. Amen.

Covenant

With this 'Mass-Credo' in mind we focus now on a favoured aspect of the Church's understanding of offering sacrifice, that of covenant renewal and covenant commitment.

At the heart of the Christian's relationship with God, into which we enter through baptism, is the 'covenant' which God has made with humankind through the cross. Not alone did Jesus inaugurate this new covenant, and seal it with his blood; he gave us a rite by which the covenant could be renewed to the end of time. That rite is the Mass. To "join Christ in offering the sacrifice" at Mass is to renew and re-commit ourselves to the covenant. It is to associate ourselves with Christ in his self-offering to the Father, to take on something of his mentality (*Ph 2:5-8*), to think and speak and live as he did, to hold on to and stand by our Christian principles amid the challenges and knocks of daily living. And to commit ourselves to the living out of this 'Way' no matter what the cost.

The best way to discover what all this involves is to listen with a yearning heart and a welcoming heart to the scripture readings at Mass, and to check our life-style in the light of those scriptures as in a mirror. Then in the eucharistic prayer we surrender to that life-style, pledging ourselves to it by the blood of Christ.

'Offering the sacrifice' has to do therefore with the mentality with which we enter into the proclamation by the priest of the eucharistic prayer. That mentality must be the mentality of Christ. Like him we pledge ourselves to be "obedient unto death, even death on a cross" (*Ph 2:8*). And we covenant ourselves to adhere to his Way, knowing that it will involve the taking up of a cross, the cross of daily living as a Christian (*Lk 9:23*).

To alert us to this mentality, and to help us maintain an attitude of praise and offering during the eucharistic prayer, the Church tells us to "listen with silent reverence" to the priest, and to join in the various acclamations (*IGMR 55*). It remains for us to look now at these acclamations which punctuate the proclamation of the eucharistic prayer. These, in the Missal,[15] come at four points:

(i). *The dialogue before the preface:* "The Lord be with you . . . Lift up your hearts . . . Let us give thanks to the Lord our God." The words summon us to an attitude of attentiveness. In a spirit of awe we lift up our hearts as if to peer into heaven.[16] It is as if the Lord is awaiting us to take up our earthly prayer into his own heavenly prayer of praise and self-offering. "Let us give thanks to the Lord our God." The eucharistic prayer does not belong exclusively to the

15. Some people, in a possible future revision of the Missal, would like to see further acclamations as in the eucharistic prayers for Masses with children, and in some eucharistic prayers of the Eastern rites. Others favour the silent listening with the acclamations as in the present Missal.

16. The image is prompted by a reading of Ronald Knox: *The Mass in Slow Motion,* Sheed and Ward, 1948, page 8.

priest; it belongs also to the faithful. Only when he has heard our word of approval "it is right to give him thanks and praise", only then will the priest embark on the proclamation of the prayer on our behalf.[17]

(ii). *"Holy, holy, holy."* With these words we break in upon the liturgy of heaven, joining with our great high priest, with all the powers of heaven, with Mary and the saints, and with our own loved ones who have gone before us – joining with them all as with one voice we sing our single victory song, our single chorus of praise.[18]

(iii). *The proclamation of the mystery of faith.* In faith and love we acclaim the Lord, proclaiming that the Christ who died for us is risen and will come again. He *died,* died for this moment when we could stand reconciled in the presence of the Father.[19] He is *risen,* alive, present in our midst, and active in our celebration. He will *come again,* at that unknown moment to which we look forward with the prayer of the ancient Church in our hearts: Come, Lord Jesus!

(iv). *Doxology and Amen.* Here the priest adds gesture to word as if to secure the faithful's utmost attention for their final acclamation, the 'great Amen'. It is a gesture of offering sacrifice. Holding aloft both host and chalice he proclaims to the world that through Christ, with Christ, and in Christ, in the unity of the holy Spirit, all glory and honour belong to God the Almighty Father for ever and ever. Into the self-offering of Jesus our praise and self-offering are subsumed. Our covenant pledge is sealed, and our great Amen becomes our great Yes to God the Father through the Son in the holy Spirit. It is our Yes of adoration and wonderment, our Yes of sorrow and petition, our Yes of gratitude. It is our Yes to life, our Yes to death, our Yes to eternity.

IV Sacramental Communion

The fourth and final aspect of eucharistic worship which we examine here in relation to the Mass as an experience of God concerns eucharistic communion. And we pose the question: what do people experience, or what ought people experience, when they "go

17. *cf* St John Chrysostom, *Homily on 2 Co 18:3.*

18. Or, with Eastern rite Christians, we can envision heaven coming down upon earth in the eucharist.

19. *cf Eucharistic Prayer,* II.

to communion?" The answer can best be summarised as follows: *holy communion is meant to be an experience of intimacy with Jesus-Eucharist, an awareness of the love-ties which bond us to our fellow Christians and our fellow humans, and a communing in the sacrifice of Jesus Christ.* Holy communion is all that, and more.

Intimacy with Jesus-Eucharist

(i) First, the communicant experiences *intimacy* with Jesus-Eucharist,[20] an intimacy which is "astonishing beyond measure."[21] To help people appreciate how deep this intimacy is the early Fathers made a comparison with the bodily union of spouses in marriage. But eucharistic communion is something far deeper: it is nothing less than the assimilation of the Lord into our very being, under the form of food and drink. In promising to give himself to us in this form Jesus uses the terms "flesh and blood", a Hebrew idiom for the whole *person.* In this way Jesus conveys to us that our union with him in the eucharist is of a deeply personal nature. And to convey something of the permanence and profundity of this union Jesus uses the term "abide", a word which is variously translated as "lives in me", "is united with me", "remains in me". On this question Jim McPolin comments: "The relationship which Jesus offers implies a permanent presence of one person to another, intimate indwelling and familiarity. Like two friends present to one another in listening, understanding and loving response, the disciple is present to Christ and Christ to the disciple."[22] The fact that communion takes the form of a physical receiving of the sacred species makes us psychologically conscious of the intimacy about which we are speaking, the intimacy of our union with Jesus.[23] Augustine speaks of our assimilation into Christ. And Thomas Aquinas speaks of our transformation into him: the proper effect of the sacrament, Thomas writes, is to transform us so much into Christ that we can

20. On the question of 'intimacy' with Jesus-Eucharist see Francis Frost in *Eucharist for a New World,* ed Seán Swayne, Irish Institute of Pastoral Liturgy, 1981.

21. *Imitation of Christ, 2:1-6.*

22. James McPolin, S.J., *John,* Veritas Publications, Dublin, 1979, page 168.

23. Frost, *op cit,* page 48. Fr John Fullenbach, at the 1986 Annual Carlow Liturgy Seminar, said: "God demonstrates his desire for unity in such a way that he wants to be physically united with us", tape 5 in the Veritas cassette of the seminar.

truly say: "I live now, not I, but Christ lives in me."[24]

The meal image of the eucharist, for that is what we have been using, is useful too from another point of view. It is an image used frequently in scripture to describe the closeness of God to his people, especially in the messianic age; for with Christ there is a new degree of closeness between God and the believer. And this closeness reaches its highpoint in sacramental communion: "Whoever eats my flesh and drinks by blood abides in me and I abide in that person."

Here reference must be made to the blessed Trinity. Through intimacy with Jesus-Eucharist we are drawn into a relationship of intimacy with the Father through the Spirit. It is the same relationship of intimacy which Jesus himself enjoys *(Jn 6:57)*. In that way holy communion transports us into the inner life of the Trinity. Into that life we are drawn in a relationship of intimate loving and listening, responding and understanding.

Union With Others

(ii) A second observation on communion as 'experience' is this. If communion is an experience of union with Jesus-Eucharist, it is also an experience, or ought to be, of our union with others: "We, many though we are, are one body, for we all partake of one loaf" (*1 Co 10:17*). One loaf, formed of many grains gathered from many hills! That was how the early Christians envisaged their union, according to the *Didaché*, a document of the first century. Which brings up, once again, the meal image. A meal bonds. A meal creates community. In this meal which is the eucharist we are bonded together in Christ, united to one another in Christ.

Communion time, therefore, is a time for awareness of others, awareness of one's fellow Christians, awareness of all God's people. It is a time when Jesus' new commandment of love should come sharply into focus, a time for community consciousness, a time for thoughts of forgiveness and caring, thoughts of loving and sharing.

Here it may be appropriate to raise a practical question in relation to the communion procession and its importance as a sign of, and means towards fostering, union among the communicants. The Missal envisages a "fraternal" procession (*IGMR, 56i*), a procession of joy-filled people, bonded together in the Lord, and singing together

24. In *IV Sent. Dist. 12, q. 2, a. 1-2.*

a single song as they move towards his table. In practice, unfortunately, it rarely reads in that way. One remedy is to have two altar servers or ministers, dressed in albs and carrying lighted candles, take up a position some distance down the central aisle during the 'Lamb of God'. Then, when the people have responded to the priest's invitation "This is the Lamb of God . . . " the servers move at processional pace towards the central distribution point, with the people falling in behind them in a double line procecession. Prior to all this the Our Father, the prayers for unity and peace, and the sign of peace will have helped towards fostering communion-awareness among the people, helping them to see themselves as one, and to be aware of the ties that bond them together in the Lord. That at least, is the hope.

Communing in Christ's Redemptive Work

(iii) Thirdly, holy communion means communing in the redemptive work of Christ, in his sacrifice, having his 'attitude' (*Ph 2:5*). It means associating ourselves with the cause for which he died,[25] renewing our commitment to a path which will lead us inevitably to a cross (*Mt 10:38*), determining to endure the cross for the sake of the joy which lies before us (*Heb 12:2*).

In this context it will be useful to draw attention to the practice in some celebrations where communicants sign themselves with the sign of the cross when they receive communion, thereby aligning themselves, through a ritual gesture, with the cross and everything it implies. It is a practice which ought to be fostered.

Receiving the chalice is another sign and reminder that participation in the eucharist involves commitment, by the blood of Christ, to the new covenant and to the Christian 'Way'.

Prefigurations in Scripture

Intimacy with Jesus-Eucharist, an awareness of the ties which bond us to one another, a sense of identifying with Christ in his self-offering – all of this is part of what Christians experience when they receive communion at Mass. But communion has other rich associations too. Drawing on the prefigurations of the eucharist in the scrip-

25. I take the expression from Dermot Ryan in *Church and Eucharist,* ed Michael Hurley, S.J., Gill and Son, Dublin and Melbourne, 1966, page 171. It is a particularly fine essay.

tures we think of communion as the manna for our desert journeying: just as the bread from heaven sustained our spiritual ancestors in the desert (*Ex 16*) so does it sustain us when life is discouraging. Communion, too, is the food which renews us when, like Elijah in hiding, we are downcast and afraid; in the strength of this food from heaven we are able to rise up and continue our journey "towards the mountain of God" (*1 K 19*). Our final example from scripture we find in Matthew 15: there we find a people hungry and weary, in danger of "collapsing on the way". We are those people. And only in the Lord, whose heart is moved to pity at our condition (*15:32*), will our desperate needs find their answer. "No one who comes to me shall ever be hungry", Jesus tells us in his discourse on the Eucharist; "no one who believes in me will ever thirst" (*Jn 6:35*).

Another aspect of the communion 'experience' to recall here is the exhilaration of knowing, on the authority of Jesus himself *(Jn 6:51)*, that communion is the pledge and the anticipation of the banquet of heaven, eternal life. "O sacred banquet! There is Christ received, the memory of his passion recalled, the mind is filled with grace, and a pledge of future glory is given to us."[26] Finally, there is the traditional comparison of communion with ordinary food and its effect upon us.[27] Food "sustains, gives growth, repairs and delights". Communion *sustains* us, protecting us from any serious lapse into grave sin. It gives spiritual *growth*, perfecting us in our effort to live the Christian life. It *repairs*, erasing our daily venial failings. It *delights*, bringing us a joy in the Lord which at times can be experienced even in one's person.

We have been considering sacramental communion in the context of our discussion of the Mass as an experience of God. That experience can be facilitated by the ambience of the church, the attitude of the congregation, the music, the ceremonial, the reverence in bearing of priest and ministers. A final responsibility rests with the eucharistic minister at the actual moment of communion. Reverence on the part of the eucharistic minister, as he or she holds the host slightly raised and pronounces the words "The body of Christ", will help to bring about reverence on the part of the communicant, and will elicit a heartfelt "Amen" of faith, of welcome, and of commitment to the Lord.

26. From the antiphon *O Sacrum Convivium*.
27. *Decree to the Armenians, Denzinger 698.*

The body of Christ. Amen!
Amen, yes. I believe. I believe this is the Lord.
    Help my unbelief.
Amen, yes. I welcome the Lord,
    coming to me at this moment,
    coming to me intimately, personally.
Amen, yes. I renew my commitment to the Lord,
    to his way, to the cross
    which he invites me to share with him.
Amen, yes. I promise to respond to his love for me,
    to radiate to other people something of his love,
    his concern, his forgiveness.
Amen, yes; I pledge myself to work
    to build up his body, the Church,
    to concern myself with his little ones in need.
Amen, yes. I open my heart to the blessed Trinity,
    Father, Son and Spirit,
    coming to me to live in me,
    to make their home in me.
Amen, yes. I look forward to eternal communion
    with my God, with all the heavenly beings,
    with Mary and the blessed,
    and with all my loved ones
    in the light, happiness and peace of heaven.

Authenticity

"The present century is thirsting for authenticity" – Pope Paul VI

To raise the question of authenticity in liturgical celebration is in no way to question the sincerity of the various ministers. To be authentic is one thing. To be seen to be authentic is another.

A visiting priest was doing supply work one Sunday in a village church in the west of Ireland. Afterwards he complimented the reader, a burly fisherman from the locality who had never gone beyond the primary school. The fisherman explained how he had prepared the reading, the famous passage on love from 1 Corinthians, chapter 13. "I have a large family, Father", he said, "and I decided at the beginning of the week to try to live what Paul said, before reading it to the people on Sunday. I tried to be 'patient, kind', to avoid being 'arrogant, rude'. The effort nearly crucified me." Recounting the story afterwards, the priest said that every word of that reading seemed to have been coloured by the fisherman's efforts during the week to live what he was going to proclaim on Sunday. The reading came across in a powerful, penetrating way. It came from the heart. It was authentic.

It was Paul VI who said that the present century is thirsting for authenticity: "Young people especially have a horror of the artificial or false. What they are searching for above all is truth and honesty."[1] To raise the question of authenticity in liturgical celebration is in no way to question the sincerity of the various ministers in the liturgy, priest or lay. The problem is that a person can be authentic without being seen to be authentic. One bishop tells how he was challenged one day in a post-primary school by a pupil who asked: "Why do so many priests not mean what they say at Mass?" Another bishop who asked a twelve year old acquaintance whose parish priest had died: "What kind of a new priest would you like?" was promptly told "One who will mean what he says when he is saying Mass."

1. *Evangelii Nuntiandi,* 1975.

Authenticity in liturgical celebration requires that the liturgy be what it purports to be. It demands that every word spoken, every gesture performed, every action carried out correspond to the reality which underlies it.

Words

The late Clifford Howell entitled one of his books *Mean What You Say.*[2] The phrase prompts a reflection on the manner in which some of the ministers of the liturgy use words. If words used at Mass are to touch the hearts of the people, they must come from the heart, "filled to the brim with authenticity".[3]

The priest. Take as an example the simple greeting at the beginning of Mass: "The Lord be with you." The priest cannot make these words come alive in the hearts of the people unless he himself understands what they mean and why he uses them. Through the greeting "the priest expresses the presence of the Lord to the assembled community" *(IGMR 28).*

The priest's task therefore, as he pronounces these words, is to try to focus the congregation's attention on the presence in their midst of the glorious risen Lord. The priest too will be aware of the biblical roots of the greeting. When great leaders and prophets like Gideon, Joshua, and Jeremiah wavered at the thought of some task facing them they were reassured: "The Lord will be with you" *(Jg 6:13; Jos 1:5; Jr 1:8).* So with us today. The God who was with Gideon, Joshua and Jeremiah in their helplessness is with us in our need, guiding, supporting and accompanying us through the Spirit of the risen Lord. This then is the priest's prayer for his people as he opens his arms and his heart to them at the beginning of Mass: "Do not be afraid. The Lord is with you, with each one of you, in your decision making, in your frailty, in your brokenness. The Lord loves you – not for what you ought to be, but for what you are now. Do not be afraid, then. You are never alone. Friends may depart from you, but the Lord is with you – in life, and in death when he will take you to the Father and to the loved ones from whom you are parted." Words thus pondered upon will come from the heart, will

2. Geoffrey Chapman, London, Dublin, 1966.

3. Tatiana Goricheva in *Talking About God Is Dangerous,* SCM Press Ltd., 1984, page 91.

touch hearts, and will add to this moment of the Eucharist a dimension of welcome, joy, peace and attentiveness.

One could continue, pondering the whole text and ritual of the Mass in this way. As he introduces the penitential rite, for example, the priest will realise that his task here is to lead the congregation into an awareness of their need for reconciliation before they offer their gift at the altar *(Mt 5:23),* and into an attitude of praise of God for his mercy. As he says "Let us pray" before the opening prayer the priest's intention will be to help the people to "be still" before God, and in the silence of their hearts put before him their personal needs. As he introduces the readings the priest will try to arouse in the hearts of the people a yearning to hear the voice of the Lord speaking to them. At the prayer of the faithful he will aim at helping the people to see themselves as a priestly people who, at this point in the Mass, exercise their priestly function of joining Christ in interceding for the Church and the world. At the dialogue before the preface "The Lord be with you . . . Lift up your hearts" the priest's words will be coloured by his awareness that the people's role in the eucharistic prayer is to take their stand alongside Christ in praising God for his wonderful works, and in offering the sacrifice (*cf IGMR 54*). At Communion time the priest's task will be to facilitate the kind of atmosphere in the church in which people will more easily experience deep personal intimacy with Jesus-Eucharist. Finally, as he reaches out to the congregation at the concluding rite of Mass, the priest will see himself as the human instrument through which Christ is sending them forth "to love and serve the Lord" and to continue breaking bread with their neighbour in need. And so for all the words of the Mass. If the priest is to give spirit to those words he will "celebrate the liturgy in such a way that he will convey an awareness of the meaning of the sacred actions" (*EM 1967, 20*). Words thus pondered upon and prayed over will take on something of that penetrating power of the word of God which is living and active and sharper than any two-edged sword *(Heb 4:12).*

The reader. "It is the message that should be remembered, not the one who reads it."[4] Authenticity on the part of the reader will require that the reader first study the passage in question, take to heart the message it contains, be committed to the living out of that word,

4. USA Bishops' Committee on the Liturgy, *Newsletter,* vol 1, No 4, 1965.

and approach the ambo with a longing to communicate a deeply felt conviction about the word. Such care for the word will register in the very bearing of the reader, in the manner in which the reading is proclaimed, and in the awareness with which the reader pauses at the conclusion before announcing: "This is the word of the Lord."[5]

In the ceremony of Institution of Readers, the bishop addresses the candidates in these words: "In proclaiming God's word to others accept it yourself in obedience to the holy Spirit. Meditate on it constantly so that each day you will have a deeper love for the scriptures, and in all you say and do show forth to the world our Saviour, Jesus Christ." These words point to the care which must go into the preparation of the reader and the readings. For the reader at the ambo is God's prophet, showing forth to the world its saviour.

The psalmist. Whenever the word is proclaimed in the liturgical assembly God reveals something of himself to us. And when God reveals himself we naturally respond. Mary's response to divine revelation was that outburst of joy, the Magnificat. Simeon's was the Nunc dimittis, Zachary's the Benedictus. Our response to divine revelation is the responsorial psalm. The challenge to the psalmist at Mass therefore is not simply to sing the psalm verses audibly and beautifully, but to articulate through the prayerfulness of his or her singing the praise, gratitude, wonderment, joy, sorrow and trust which well up in the hearts of the people present. The psalmist's role then is to lead the congregation into an attitude of inner prayer, to sing the psalm in such a way that it will create a prayer-filled resonance in the hearts of the hearers. And this is a skill which the psalmist will acquire only through prayer.

The congregation. With regard to the authenticity of the congregation's responses, we take as an example the response at the end of the eucharistic prayer, the great Amen. That Amen is a powerful, glorious and majestic moment of the liturgy, the people's moment par excellence. Through it they ratify everything the priest has said and done. In that tiny word is concentrated and expressed all their adoration of God, all their gratitude, all their sorrow, all their needs. In it too is contained their offering of their daily lives to God, their solemn renewal of their covenant pledge to live as children of

5. "Ministry in the liturgy is inseparable from the whole of life. One cannot be foul-mouthed or untruthful in daily life, and then rise in the assembly of the faithful to proclaim the word believably" – *Liturgy* 80, May 1983, page 4.

him who said: I will be their God, and they shall be my people. People who thus understand the great Amen, and who are told repeatedly that the Church wants them to sing it once again as in the days of Justin and Jerome, can scarely be blamed for questioning the authenticity of a celebration if they find the great Amen replaced by a great mumble. "Jerome tells us how the great Amen used sound like a thunder clap in the ancient basilicas. Merely to speak the word is to do less than justice to its majesty and power. It must be sung. Through song, and the prolongation and repetition which it permits, we are able to express our Amen more beautifully and ponder more at length on its meaning."[6] A sung Amen is an authentic Amen.

We leave the final word about authenticity in words to Tatiana Goricheva, a brilliant young Russian student living in Leningrad, who became a Christian and moved to the West when the KGB caught up with her. In her story, *Talking About God is Dangerous* (SCM Press Ltd, 1984) she speaks of the first time she listened to a religious broadcast on television, after coming to the West: "What this man said on the screen was likely to drive more people out of the church than the clumsy chatter of our paid atheists . . . For the first time I understood how dangerous it is to talk about God. Each word is a sacrifice, filled to the brim with authenticity. Otherwise it is better to keep silent" (pp 90-1).

Gestures

Gestures must speak. Authenticity in gesture requires that gestures correspond to the reality which underlies them. To illustrate the point we consider three gestures. The first is that which accompanies the opening greeting, "The Lord be with you." The rubrics direct: "The priest, facing the people, extends his hands and greets all present." However, if there is to be authenticity of gesture, much more will be required than mere compliance with the rubrics. The hands will reach out in a gesture which is shaped by an understanding of what one is doing at that precise moment, welcoming and gathering the people, and reminding them of the Lord's presence in their midst. Similarly at the epiclesis: "The priest joins his hands and, holding them outstretched over the offerings, says:

6. Seán Swayne, *Communion, the New Rite of Mass*, Veritas 1974, page 65-66.

'Let your Spirit come upon these gifts . . .' "[7] Here the priest will somehow try to evoke the coming down of the Spirit through a full unhurried reaching out of the hands and arms at shoulder height, followed by a 'descending' movement towards the offerings. A final example is the gesture which accompanies the words: "The peace of the Lord be with you always." The rubric simply says: "The priest extends and joins his hands." But those outstretched hands must speak of a pleading for peace and a fraternal reaching out of the heart towards one's brothers and sisters. At the same time the gesture will convey the priest's own at-ease-ness and peace of soul which he longs to share with the congregation.

Actions

Actions too should speak, but so often in practice they fail to do so. The procession with the gifts, more commonly (and less accurately) called 'the offertory procession' is an example. Frequently it comes across as little more than an awkward physical transferring of the bread and wine from point A to point B in the church. If the procession with the gifts is to be authentic, then those carrying the bread and wine and water will carry them in such a way that they convey an awareness of what their action signifies: it is an expression of the people's active part in the Mass, and a public reverencing of the elements which are symbols of God's gifts of life and nourishment, destined to become our spiritual food and drink. The communion procession too leaves room for development. Few churches seem to carry out the procession in the manner the missal envisages it, as "an act of brotherhood and sisterhood" (*IGMR, 56i*). Instead, one witnesses in the average church in Ireland a purely functional converging of a crowd towards the point of distribution of hosts. Like gestures, liturgical actions are ritual rather than functional, and the ritualised procession at Communion should speak of a people on pilgrimage, moving towards the Lord in a fellowship of love, "their voices joined in a single song" (*56i*).

Objects

In the liturgy we reach out to God through material elements. Bread, wine, fire and light become our points of contact with the

7. *Eucharistic Prayer,* II.

divinity. Here too we must check for authenticity.[8] The bread used in the eucharist – and the point has been made repeatedly since 1970 when the Roman Missal stated that "the nature of the sign demands that the material for the eucharistic celebration appear as actual food" *(IGMR 283)* – ought to look like bread, even though unleavened.

In this connection, Maria Boulding makes an interesting observation: "In my community we use at Mass hosts baked from wholemeal flour. They are not the smooth, uniform, thin, white wafers of earlier days. They have a beautiful homespun roughness about them. Not a single host is perfect, and no two hosts are alike. There are speckled ones, dark ones, chipped ones, flawed ones. There are rough ones with little excrescences and cracks – a perfect picture of a community! And yet none are scorned or rejected when carried to the sanctuary. Christ graciously accepts them, to turn them into his body."[9]

The scented smoke of the incense ought to be seen, and smelled. Candles ought to burn with a flame that is real, not imitative. Vestments ought to be graceful, and contemporary. Lectionaries and Gospel-books ought to express our reverence for God's word. Jugs, basins and towels ought to replace the miniature substitutes which we have grown used to at the washing of the hands. All through, the counterfeit must give way to the authentic.

Church furnishings

Too often the furnishings reflect a casualness in our approach to God far removed from the traditional attitude which sees God as the *rex tremendae maiestatis,* the God of indescribable majesty. A church is a sacred place, and the manner in which it is arranged "greatly contributes to a worthy celebration and to the

8. "There is a growing desire in our country that the signs, symbols, gestures and other elements be more genuine so that their very authenticity may lead worshippers to a truer understanding of and faith in what they are doing in liturgy. The controversy over eucharistic bread in our country was symptomatic of that yearning for authenticity. Signs and symbols as well as liturgical texts bear the Church's tradition . . . Renewal requires the opening up of our symbols, especially the fundamental ones of bread and wine, water, oil, the laying-on of hands, until we can experience all of them as authentic and appreciate their symbolic use." (from the report of the USA Bishops' Committee on the Liturgy at the world convention of national liturgy commissions in Rome, 23-27 October, 1984).

9. *New Liturgy,* No 31, page 8.

active participation of the people" *(EM 24)*. The church and its furnishings should somehow speak of the beauty of God and of the splendour of the liturgy. The chair should be designed in a manner which expresses its importance as the chair of Christ, ie, of the priest who presides over the faithful in the person of Christ. The ambo too will be beautifully designed and constructed, reflecting the dignity of the word of God. The altar should inspire people with a sense of wonderment at the sacred mysteries enacted upon it. And so on for all the furnishings. People today are more sensitive to the visual than before. They reject the phoney, the sham, and the garish. In everything they seek authenticity.

Silence

A dead silence makes no sense. A short stoppage to comply with a rubric after the "Let us call to mind our sins" or the "Let us pray" before the Collect is a far cry from the kind of silence which the liturgy envisages, "which allows the voice of the Spirit to be heard more fully in our hearts" *(IGHL 202)*. Silence in the liturgy is a time for pondering, like Mary, in the heart *(Lk 2:19)*. We pause at the penitential rite to focus on our need for reconciliation with God and with one another, and to praise him who forgives, even though our sins be as scarlet *(Is 1:18)*. At the Collect we commune silently with the Lord as we put before him our deeply felt personal needs. Following the readings we enter into the inner sanctum of our hearts to ponder God's message and apply it to our lives. As the gifts are being prepared, we prepare silently for the eucharistic prayer, when we will praise the Father and offer ourselves to him, together with Christ. During the communion silence we pause to savour those golden moments of intimate communion with Jesus-Eucharist.

Mass is a swift moving action. Without these moments of silence to punctuate the celebration, our participation risks resting at a merely external level. And liturgy which is merely external is an empty shell. The silences provided by the revised Roman Missal are to be welcomed therefore as rich moments during which we can interiorise the mystery we celebrate.

"The present generation, young people particularly, are thirsting for authenticity." In them Christ is thirsting. It is on the priest and those who exercise a ministry in the eucharistic celebration that the duty of giving them to drink *(Jn 4:7)* primarily rests.

Joy in the Mass

"When the Church lost her joy she lost the world" – Alexander Schmemann.

The joy which ought to characterise the life and personality of the Christian ought also permeate the entire celebration of the Eucharist.

I am writing these reflections on the feast of the great Anthony of Egypt, father of monasticism. Athanasius, the biographer of Anthony, tells us that "strangers knew him among his disciples by the joy on his face." Another biographer, Adomnan, makes a similar observation about his subject, Columba: "His holy face was always cheerful, and in his innermost heart he was happy with the joy of the holy Spirit."[1]

On reflection one would expect that the same claim could be made for every Christian. For Christians are resurrection people: "We are an Easter people and Alleluia is our song!" (Augustine). Each of us knows that God *is;* that he has called me by my name, and has my name branded on the palm of his hand *(Is 49:6);* that he loves me, loves me not as I ought to be, but as I am – personally, intimately, infinitely; that he is with me at every instant as I go my pilgrim way through life. Joy comes from having Mary for my Mother,[2] and the Church for my guide; it comes from knowing that when I am oppressed by sin or sickness the gifts of God's forgiveness and healing are there for the taking; it comes from my weekly and even daily nourishment on the bread of the word and bread of the eucharist; it comes from knowing that whatever suffering comes by way in life has a redemptive value, and cannot be compared with the glory which is to come; it comes from knowing that death is not the end, that partings from loved ones are only for a time, and that the

1. Office of Readings for feast of St Columba, 9 June.

2. *cf* Paul VI's Apostolic Exhortation *On Christian Joy,* 9 May 1975.

end of my life on earth signals my victorious pass-over to my Father in heaven.

The reality, unfortunately, can be different, and at times people search in vain among Christians for the joy which bearers of the Good News ought to radiate. In fact, according to Nietzsche, Christians are lacking in joy. And the same writer made one of the cruelest accusations ever levelled against the Church when he said that the Church was trying to rob people of their joy. Commenting on Nietzsche, Alexander Schmemann, the great Orthodox theologian, said that when the Church lost her joy she lost the world.[3] The "losing" goes on in our own day. When husbands and wives lose their joy they lose each other. When religious communities lose their joy they lose their postulants. When priests lose their joy they lose the hearts of the young men who might have followed them into the priesthood.[4]

Joy in the Bible.

In the bible joy is a key word. God's revelation of himself arouses an intense joy in the human heart. Joy seizes us when we advert to the goodness of God and his wonderful works throughout history. The heavens rejoice in the presence of God, Isaiah tells us. So too the earth, even the wasteland *(52:9)*. The bible speaks frequently of the ordinary joys of human living: wine *(Ps 104)*, the love of a wife *(Pr 5:19)*, the sky at night *(Ps 8)*; all are God's gift to us. Biblical joy finds its most powerful expression in ths psalms: "Come, ring out our joy in the Lord . . . Shout for joy . . . The Lord is our help and our shield, in him do our hearts find joy" *(Ps 95:1; 149:5; 33:21)*.

In the New Testament the note of joy intensifies. Luke's Gospel opens and closes in a mood of joy. The angel's greeting to Mary sets the tone: "Rejoice, O favoured one" *(1:28)*. In the presence of the unborn saviour the Baptist leaps for joy in the womb of his mother *(1:44)*. Mary's response to divine revelation is an outburst of joy, the Magnificat *(1:46)*. The birth of Jesus is announced to the shepherds as "good news of great joy" *(2:11)*. On the same note Luke eventual-

3. See Kallistos Ware, *The Orthodox Way,* Mowbrays, 1979, page 112.

4. "Priests should draw the hearts of young men to the priesthood by the example of their humble, happy and hardworking lives." *Decree on the Training of Priests,* par 2, Vatican II Documents.

ly closes his narrative after the ascension: "They worshipped him, and returned to Jerusalem with great joy" *(24:52)*.

So too for the other books of the New Testament. A note of joy pervades the *Acts:* the apostles rejoice that they are counted worthy to suffer for Jesus *(5:41);* Philip, having baptised the eunuch, goes on his way rejoicing *(8:39);* Barnabas rejoices when he sees the grace of God at work in Antioch *(11:23);* the Gentiles rejoice when Paul and Barnabas bring them the Gospel *(13:48)*. References to joy abound in Paul, especially in Philippians: "Rejoice in the Lord always, again I say rejoice" *(4:4)*. And even the stern Peter observes that the joy of his followers is "indescribable" *(1 Pe 1:8)*.

Gospel joy is encapsulated above all in the person of Jesus. Frequently he mentions it, for example in *Jn 15:* "These things I have spoken to you that my joy may be in you, and your joy may be full" *(v 11)*. This same joy Jesus envisions for us, his followers *(cf* also *Jn 17:13)*.

The joy which we Christians ought to experience in our personality, and in turn radiate to others, is not to be confused with feelings of wellbeing and euphoria, although such can result from it. One can be broken with grief or suffering and yet give evidence of a joy within. For joy, Gospel joy, is akin to inner peace. It is something this world cannot give. It is a gift of the Spirit *(Ga 5:22)*.

Joy in the liturgy of the early Christians.

The same joy which characterised the lives of the first Christians likewise characterised their liturgies. We have noted how after the ascension they returned with joy to Jerusalem and were continually blessing God in the temple *(Lk 24:52-3)*. Soon afterwards we find them breaking bread in their homes with joyfilled and generous hearts *(Ac 2:46)*. *Hebrews* is further evidence of the festive quality of the early Christian liturgies: "You have come to Mount Sion, and to the city of the living God, the heavenly Jerusalem, and to innumerable angels in festal gathering" *(12:22)*. Later in the writings of the apologists the same joy-filled festive quality of the Christian liturgy is echoed: Ignatius of Antioch, for example, writing about 105 refers to the liturgical assembly gathered "in irreproachable joy . . . rejoicing . . . and glorifying the Name."[5]

So it was therefore in the beginning. So it must be again. Every

5. Letter to the Magnesians 7 and Philippians 10.

eucharist should vibrate with joy and festivity, for every eucharist is a victory celebration, the celebration of Christ's victory and our victory over sin and death. In the eucharist we hold aloft before the eyes of the world the glorious Cross on which hung the Saviour. We proclaim with joy, with intense joy, that the One who died on that Cross is risen, alive, and will come again. When we celebrate the eucharist we celebrate in the joy of thanksgiving our liberation from sin and death, our reconciliation with the creator, our gratitude to him who so loved the world.

"Be joyful always on Sunday" was the cry of the early Christians, echoed in the third century writing, the *Didascalia Apostolorum*. The same work tells us that to do penance on Sunday is a sin (we are still in the third century!) so incompatible is penance with the spirit of joy which ought to mark the Sunday assembly.[6] Today we not only recognise the place of joy in our Sunday eucharist. We pray for it. "Visit us Lord this night," we pray at Compline on Saturday, "so that by your strength we may rise at daybreak to rejoice in the resurrection of your Son." And when morning comes we pray again that Christ "will bring us to share with joy this Sunday's eucharist." Nor is this a new emphasis. The old tridentine Mass began with the words: "Introibo ad altare Dei . . . I will go unto the altar of God, the God who gives joy to my youth." And that reference to joy was made even in the funeral Mass.[7] So too today in every Mass without exception there are references to joy, eg, in the embolism "Deliver us Lord from every evil . . . as we wait in joyful hope . . ."; and in the invitation to Communion: "Happy are those who are called to his Supper."

6. Connolly, *Didascalia Apostolorum,* Oxford 1969, page 192.

7. The joy which the liturgy speaks of in the funeral liturgy is in no way incompatible with human grief, as should be clear from what has already been said about Christian joy. To be joyful is Christian; to grieve is human. The liturgy must make place for grief in the funeral celebration, for to stifle it can have dangerous psychological effects. Christian joy in the face of death has to do with an inner peace which comes from knowing that death is not the end, that parting from one we love is only for a time, and that ultimately all things will be restored in Christ. It is in this sense that the Preface of Christian Death can say "In our joy we sing to your glory."

The point is illustrated in the incident of Martin Luther clasping to himself his dying daughter Magdalena: "Dear little Leni, you will rise and shine like the stars and the sun" he cried. And he added, "how strange to know that she is at peace and all is well, and yet to be so full of grief" *(Tablet, 12 November 1983, p 1105).*

Speaking of the 'atmosphere of joy' which characterises every Mass, Pope John Paul II says: "Even though we are commemorating the drama of Calvary, marked out at one moment by great sadness, the priest and faithful rejoice in uniting their offering to that of Christ, because they know that they are at the same time living the mystery of the resurrection which is inseparable from this offering."[8]

Why the Eucharist is Joyous.

Joy, we have already noted, is a gift of the Spirit. Only through the Spirit will joy find its way into our celebration of the Mass. It comes from pondering on the wondrous intimacy with which God invites us, sinners though we are, to his sacred banquet. It comes from listening with a yearning and receptive heart to the word which God speaks in the scriptures: "When I found your words I devoured them; they became my joy, and the happiness of my heart" *(Jr 15:16)*. It comes from knowing that when we join Christ in the eucharistic prayer in thanking the Father for redemption, for the faith, for life and health, our thanks is divinised, deified, and subsumed into Christ's own prayer to the Father. It comes from the "earnestness" *(cf Lk 22:15)* with which we desire to join Christ in the offering of his Sacrifice. It comes from savouring the intimacy with which the Lord unites himself with us in sacramental communion. It comes from the eagerness with which we wait in joyful hope for the coming of our Saviour at the end. It comes from an awareness that Mass is a breaking in upon the heavenly liturgy,[9] a coming down of heaven on earth, an activity in which we are joined by Mary, by "the saints and angels" (Preface) and by our own loved ones who are now with God in heaven.

Christian joy, therefore, must somehow find clear and vibrant expression in the eucharist. The entire celebration should capture, reflect and express that joy. Music, song, ceremonial, lights, vestments, processions, incensations, the physical setting – all should combine to facilitate the kind of atmosphere which such a celebration calls for. In that way the Gospel joy latent in the hearts of the people will register in the celebration, and the joy of the celebration will in turn vibrate in the hearts of the people.

8. *General Audience,* 8 June 1983.

9. See later chapter *The Heavenly Liturgy.*

Externals

"The person who tries to become an angel becomes an ass" – Pascal.

Worship which is purely internal is not only undesirable; it is impossible. It is through the externals of worship that the celebration speaks to the faithful, for good or for ill.

Mireille Nègre, the celebrated dancer of the Paris Opera, entered a Carmelite convent in 1971. In her book *Je Danserai Pour Toi,*[1] she writes with affection of her years in the cloister. Carmel was her school of prayer *par excellence.* But a problem arose. Gradually the body with which God had gifted her became "an icicle of frustration". She writes: "In the liturgy we would chant the psalm 'I will dance for you, O Lord, around the altar', but while I pronounced the words my body remained fixed and rigid, motionless as a marble statue, betraying not even the faintest trace of joy, the joy about which the psalm spoke . . . this duality between body and soul left me diminished." And so in 1981 Mireille left the community she loved to devote her life to dancing for the glory of God. "My dream is to bring my dancing into the hospitals, the prisons, wherever there is suffering and pain and loneliness. I want to bring to them the dance of Jesus' smile." And she adds: "The Church, with its vast body of so many members, will always need the heart of the contemplatives, the spirit of the learned, the hand of the active workers like the admirable Mother Teresa, the feet of the missionaries, the tongue of the poets, the bodies of the sick, the blood of the martyrs. But the Church will always need too the sensitiveness of the artist." After she left Carmel, Mireille made a sensational appearance on French television where she danced Vivaldi's Gloria. Afterwards a viewer wrote: "You must go with your dancing into the hospitals and prisons. There you will win souls. You must go into the churches which today are deserted. If you do, thousands of people will return, not to assist at the spectacle, but to pray with you."

1. Desclée de Brouwer, 1984.

The Body in Worship

Some people have little time for the externals of worship. Singing and ceremonial, studied gestures and processions, well designed furnishings and concern about the niceties of the physical setting – all belong to the outer shell, the periphery of worship. What matters, they contend, is one's inner attitude.

To argue thus is fallacy. It is true that worship ought to be primarily internal. But not solely internal. In fact purely internal worship is impossible because of the union of the material and the spiritual within us. "Prayer cannot happen without the body," writes André Louf; "our body plays a central role in the return to the Father with Jesus in the Spirit. Every prayer, however secret and however interior it may be, will be mirrored in the body."[2]

Archbishop Rembert G. Weakland, OSB, points out in his *All God's People*[3] that the accent in liturgy after Vatican II was on "words, words, words". But the greatest weakness was the insensitivity to the other senses: "Since people worship with all their being, all senses come into play. Liturgy should not be triumphal or pompous, but it must appeal to the eye and nose and ear without being Hollywoodish or maudlin. That is the challenge."

Worship must engage us therefore in the totality of our being, body as well as spirit.[4] It cannot be confined to the *inner sanctum*. Body and spirit are not separate, juxtaposed elements but principles of a single reality. If in practice this has scarcely been recognised in recent centuries it is because of the dualist philosophy of Descartes and the ancient Greeks who saw body and spirit as separate entities. Western society as a result has tended to be reprehensive of the body and elevative of the spirit. Today, happily, attitudes are changing and the human person is beginning to be seen, as Thomas Aquinas and the Hebrews saw us, in the totality of our being and personality, a *totus homo*.

So, when we come before God in worship we come before him as he came before us, enfleshed.[5] We come before him not only as peo-

2. *Teach Us To Pray,* Darton, Longman and Todd, 1974.
3. Paulist Press, New York, 1985, pages 137-8.
4. For this discussion I have found helpful Verheul: *Introduction to the Liturgy,* Anthony Clarke Books, 1969; and Martimort: *The Church at Prayer,* vol 1, Irish University Press, 1968.
5. An expression I take from Monsignor J. D. Crichton.

ple who can will and think (spiritual activities), but who can speak and sing, play, dance and celebrate (bodily activities). In worship as in life generally "the glory of God is man and woman fully alive."[6]

We must not, therefore, and we cannot attempt to stifle bodily expression of our inner attitudes when we come to worship God. Bodily prayer – words, song, stillness; postures, gestures, movement; actions such as the kissing of the cross, the holding of a candle, the signing with ashes – these not only express but foster inner attitudes of prayer. So, for example, when we genuflect in the presence of the the blessed Sacrament as an expression of our faith, the very act of genuflecting in turn fosters that faith. In other words, we pray through our bodies, because we are humans, not angels. And a person who tries to become an angel, according to Pascal, becomes an ass!

Bearing all this in mind one can appreciate the Church's insistence about the role of the entire person in worship: "Active participation should be above all internal, in the sense that by it the faithful join their minds to what they pronounce or hear, and co-operate with heavenly grace. But is should also be external, expressing internal participation through gestures and bodily attitudes, acclamations, responses and singing" *(MS 15)*.

The Physical Setting

If 'externals' are a necessary part of worship then the physical setting for and preparation of the celebration are important. Here we have a precedent from Jesus himself. One gets the impression from the Gospels that he took meticulous care to set the scene for his own preaching and worship. One could instance the care with which he prepared the great throng for the miracle of the loaves and fishes, the choice of a grassy piece of ground, and the arranging of the seating of the people in ordered groups of fifties and hundreds *(Mk 6:4)*. Again there are the precautions which he took whenever he foresaw a big attendance for his lakeside discourses – the provision of a fishing boat to prevent the crowds pressing upon him and the studied adoption of a seating posture as he spoke to them *(Mk 3:9; 4:1)*. One recalls too his concern for detail in the preparation for the final Supper. And lastly, that superb instance of his ability to create a

6. "Gloria Dei vivens homo" – Irenaeus.

listening atmosphere through his bearing and approach when he preached in the synagogue of Nazareth: "He came to Nazara . . . he went into the synagogue . . . he stood up to read . . . and there was given to him the scroll of the prophet Isaiah. He unfolded the scroll, found the place where it is written 'The Spirit of the Lord is upon me . . .' He folded up the scroll, gave it back to the attendant, and sat down. And the eyes of all were fixed upon him" *(Lk 4:16-20).*

The Need for Care

From what we have been saying it should be evident that the pastoral effectiveness of a eucharistic celebration is related to the care with which we handle the externals of worship. No degree of personal piety on the part of the presiding priest can compensate for his neglect of the external dimension.[7] If it is his duty to ensure that the faithful take part fully aware of what they are doing, actively engaged in the rite and enriched by it *(SC 11),* it is also his duty to concern himself with the external dimension too, taking care with his manner of speaking, his bearing, his gestures, his movements; taking care too with the entire physical setting: altar appointments, sanctuary, furnishings, artistic and architectural environment; taking care with the preparation of the ministers; and planning the ceremony in such a way as to take sensitive account of the nature and circumstances of the particular assembly. As the much quoted statement of the USA Bishops' Conference puts it: "Good celebrations of the liturgy nourish and strenghten faith; poor celebrations of liturgy weaken and destroy faith." It is through the externals of worship that such celebrations speak to the faithful, for good or for ill.[8]

A note on Postures at Mass

Is uniformity in the postures of people at Mass desirable? On the one hand freedom to adopt the postures most conducive to one's prayer, whether sitting, kneeling or standing, would seem to be part

7. See discussion of relevant material in chapters on *Reverence* and *Authenticity.*

8. The point is illustrated in two remarks made to me by parishioners while I was actually writing this chapter. A few days ago we introduced the use of large, thick hosts which can be broken and shared at Mass. "It makes us all feel one, Father," a parishioner commented. Also, we re-routed the entrance procession to Mass so as to pass through part of the congregation. This elicited the remark: "We feel drawn into the Mass now." Both, examples of the catechetical value of signs, of how signs speak.

of the liberty of the children of God. On the other hand one must remember that at Mass we worship not as individuals, but as a community, a people conscious of our identity as the 'People of God'. Uniformity of posture is both conducive to and an expression of orderly communal worship and of the unity of the Christian assembly, who worship with "one heart and soul" *(Ac 4:32)*.

A second question arises in relation to the postures found in different congregations. Many will have experienced the awkwardness and distraction which follows when one does not know when to kneel, stand or sit in church. It happens for instance at funerals in a strange church; sometimes an embarrassingly comical situation can arise when those in the front pews are left standing not knowing that the people behind have quietly knelt down.

Uniformity in posture would appear therefore to be desirable. And it is in fact what the Church envisages: "A common posture, observed by all, is a sign of the unity of the assembly and its sense of community. It both expresses and fosters the inner spirit and purpose of those who take part in it" *(IGMR 20)*.

The *Instruction* goes on to indicate the postures to be adopted at Mass *(20)*, adding that each conference of bishops may adapt them to the usage of their own people, taking care however that such adaptations "correspond to the character and meaning of each part of the celebration".

The postures for Mass as determined by the Irish bishops are given below. They first appeared in *The Sacraments, a Pastoral Directory,*[9] but seem to have gone largely unnoticed. An explanation of the different postures follows.

Introductory Rites

Entrance	
Greeting	
Penitential Rite	STAND
Kyrie, Gloria	
Opening Prayer	

9. Ed Seán Swayne, Veritas, 1974.

Liturgy of the Word

First Reading Responsorial Psalm Second Reading	SIT
Alleluia/Acclamation Gospel	STAND
Homily	SIT
Credo Prayer of the Faithful	STAND

Liturgy of the Eucharist

Preparation of the Gifts Orate Fratres Prayer over the Gifts	SIT
Eucharistic Prayer, from Preface to the Great Amen, inclusive	KNEEL or, in special circumstances, stand
Communion rite from Our Father	STAND
Prayer after Communion	STAND
(Notices)	SIT
Final greeting, blessing and dismissal	STAND

Standing: This is the basic liturgical posture in Christian tradition. It is a sign of respect: we stand to honour certain occasions, eg, national anthem, gospel. It is essentially a paschal posture, expressing the liberty of the Christian who has been lifted up from slavery. That is why it was forbidden in the early Church, and still is among some Eastern rite Catholics, to kneel on Sunday or during paschaltide: kneeling was considered to be out of keeping with the spirit of joy which ought to characterise Christian worship at these times. "The practice of not kneeling down during Sunday is a symbol of the resurrection by which we have been liberated, thanks to Christ, from sin and death" (St Irenaeus, fragment 7, tract on Easter). Standing was the characteristic posture for prayer among the early Christians, as the iconography of the catacombs suggests. Standing at Mass today is a sign of the faithful's active involvement, with the presiding priest who is himself standing, in the offering of the sacrifice.

In practice standing for the whole eucharistic prayer in certain places can be difficult, especially when one takes into consideration the design of pews, with kneelers which would make the act of standing somewhat torturous. The Irish bishops direct that we kneel for the eucharistic prayer (see above), ie, "from preface to the great Amen, inclusive". Sometimes one sees people sitting during the preface, then kneeling after the Sanctus – a practice which indicates that people do not realise that the entire eucharistic prayer is a unit, not to be broken, eg, by a change of posture; and that the entire eucharistic prayer, including therefore the preface, is consecratory. Consistency would demand that if we are going to kneel after the preface we should kneel during the preface; the same reverence ought to be shown during the preface as after it. In special circumstances, the Irish directives say, we may stand for the eucharistic prayer.

Sitting: This is the posture of the listener. One recalls, for example, the incident of Mary sitting at the feet of Jesus listening to his words *(Lk 10:39)*. Hence the posture of sitting as we listen to God's word at Mass. During the preparation of the gifts too we sit, as we quietly prepare ourselves for the great eucharistic prayer.

Kneeling: This posture, in Christian tradition, has a twofold significance. It is a sign of penance and compunction, the posture of a person "thrown to the ground by sin".[10] It is also a posture associated with individual prayer, especially, in more recent centuries, prayer before the blessed Sacrament *(cf Dn 6:10; Lk 22:41)*.

10. St Basil: *Tract on the holy Spirit,* 27.

The Heavenly Liturgy

"Above, angels in brilliance burst forth in the singing of the *Trisagion;* below, mortals send back the echo of their song" – John Chrysostom.

An awareness of the union between the heavenly liturgy and our own 'mortal' liturgy is a characteristic of Eastern Christian spirituality, as it was, in past generations, of Irish spirituality. The underlying doctrine is deserving of more attention.

One Sunday when I was on supply work at Raheen church, Offaly I was struck by the recollection of the local people as they gathered in the churchyard before Mass to pray at the graves of their dead. Underlying this beautiful custom is a profound theology. Mass time is a privileged moment for remembering our dead. And not only in order to intercede for them. At Mass we enter into communion with our dead. I speak of the dead whose purgation is over, and who are now with God in heaven; with them we become one in worshipping our heavenly Father. Never are we so close to our dead as when we are at Mass. For whenever Mass is celebrated there heaven is present. There God is. And Mary. And the "great multitude" of the Apocalypse *(7:9)* — visible, however, only to the eyes of faith. There at Mass are all the heavenly participants (irrespective of whether our church is full or empty)[1] – the "innumerable angels in festal gathering" *(Heb 12:23),* the saints and our own loved ones who are now, we pray, with God. At Mass, as our fellow Christians of the Eastern rite put it so tellingly, "heaven comes down upon earth".

Heaven and Earth, One in the Liturgy

This beautiful and central Christian truth, about the union between our earthly liturgy and that of heaven, seems to get scant attention from spiritual writers, retreat directors and Mass commen-

1. See Max Thurian: *L'Homme Moderne et La Vie Spirituelle,* les Presses De Taizé, 1973, page 132.

tators at the present time. Little notice seems to have been given to the statement in the *Liturgy Constitution* of 1963 which said that "in the earthly liturgy we take part in a foretaste of that heavenly liturgy which is celebrated in the holy city of Jerusalem towards which we journey as pilgrims; there with all the warriors of the heavenly army we sing a hymn of the Lord's glory." Or, to the emphasis in *Lumen Gentium, par 50,* on the union between Mass and "the worship of the heavenly Church". Or, to the reference to the heavenly liturgy in the *General Instruction on the Liturgy of the Hours,* 1971 which pointed out that in the divine Office – and the same holds for the Mass – we stand before God's throne offering praise and joining in that canticle which is sung throughout all ages in the halls of heaven *(pars 15 and 16)*.

And yet, no celebration of the eucharist takes place without a powerful reminder in the Preface that heaven and earth are one in the liturgy. Gathered around the altar we join our voices with the choirs of angels *together* proclaiming the praises of God with our Holy! Holy! Holy! The rich collection of 83 Prefaces in our present Missal gives beautiful expression, each in its own manner, to this same idea. "Earth unites with heaven . . . voices blend . . . we join the angels, the saints and the whole company of heaven . . . singing with one voice the new song of creation." At Mass we are "already with Christ in heaven", as Augustine put it: "Christ while in heaven is also with us. And we, while on earth, are also with him."[2]

Eastern Christians

This beautiful doctrine comes easily to Eastern Christians, as it did to Irish Catholics of an earlier age. Look at the liturgy as celebrated in any Greek or Russian church. There one can almost experience physically the heavenly quality which is so lamentably absent from many celebrations of the liturgy in the West. Lights, vestments, icons, chants, processions and incensations – all combine to project into their humble handling of the sacred mysteries some faint glimpse of the liturgy of heaven. "Above, the angelic armies give glory; below, in the Church, mortals are grouped together to take up after them the same hymn of praise. Above, angels in brilliance burst forth in the singing of the thrice holy hymn; below, mortals send back the echo of their song. Heavenly powers and earthly mortals are

2. *Liturgy of the Hours,* vol 2, page 627.

united in the one celebration of a single thanksgiving, a single victory song, a single chorus of joy."[3]

Timothy Ware, now Bishop Kallistos Ware, draws attention in his *The Orthodox Church* to the story of how Vladimir, prince of Kiev, while still a pagan, sent his followers in search of the true religion. Among the moslem Bulgars of the Volga they found no joy in their worship, only "mournfulness and great smell". Worship in Germany and in Rome, they found, lacked beauty. Finally they journeyed to Constantinople, and after attending the liturgy in Saint Sophia they declared: "We knew not whether we were in heaven or on earth, for surely there is no such splendour or beauty anywhere upon earth."[4]

Early Irish Liturgy

A similar awareness of the heavenly quality of the liturgy seems to have characterised the Irish of earlier centuries. Indications are to be found in the *Leabhar Breac* in the two passages, for example, to which Father Diarmuid Ó Laoghaire, S.J., draws attention in his article 'The Eucharist in Irish Spirituality'.[5] "What believer doubts that at the raising of his voice by the priest at the sacrifice heaven opens and the choirs of angels come down there, and the heavenly and earthly Church are joined and united." And again, "The elevation of the chalice of the Mass and the paten by the hands of the priest is a figure of the gathering into one fold of the people of heaven and earth: the people of heaven by the paten, the people of earth by the chalice."

Ultimately, Only One Liturgy

To appreciate the relationship of the eucharist to the heavenly liturgy one must keep in mind that there is not here a question of two liturgies, one anticipating the other, one preceding the other chronologically, one a liturgy of earth and the other a liturgy of heaven.[6] No, both liturgies are identical – as far as their substance is

3. John Chrysostom, *On Ozias, Homily 4, 1 PG 56, 120.* I found this beautiful text in Olivier Clément: *Sources, Les Mystiques Chrétiens des Origines,* Editions Stock, 1982, page 106. From the same author I borrow the term 'resurrection-space'.

4. Penguin Books, 1975, page 269.

5. *Doctrine and Life,* December 1982.

6. Helpful references: H. de Sainte-Marie: 'Liturgie de la Terre et du Ciel' in *La Maison Dieu,* No. 73; A. G. Martimort: 'L'Assemblée Liturgique, Mystère du Christ' in *La Maison Dieu,* No. 40; I. H. Dalmais: *Introduction to the Liturgy,* page 49, Geoffrey Chapman, London.

concerned; only in externals do they differ. Ultimately therefore there is only one liturgy, in which heaven and earth are united around the person of the one great High-Priest, in a single act of worship. Our liturgy here below, like the heavenly liturgy above, is nothing more than the continuation of that unique offering made once for all *(Heb 10:10)* by Jesus Christ and now perpetuated in a resurrection-space, outside the bounds of time and space. Into that resurrection-space, where there is no longer separation between earth and heaven, angels and mortals, living and dead, Mass admits us, opening for us a door into heaven *(cf Rv 4:1)*,[7] lifting us up to the level of the eternal.

To sum up: at Mass we somehow step outside the terrestrial and become part of that timeless worship offered eternally by the Son before his Father's throne in heaven. Mass is a breaking in upon, and a participation in, this one heavenly liturgy, this single chorus of joy. Constraints of time and space are lifted, and Christian mortals penetrate into eternity. All, of course, as we are painfully aware, takes place behind a veil. Owing to our earth-bound condition we join in the heavenly liturgy behind the veil of sign and symbol. Death for the Christian – Sister Death – is the removal of that veil. It is the signal for admission into the blessed Vision and face to face worship of our Abba Father in heaven.

7. See André Louf: *La Voie Cistercienne,* Desclée 1980, page 157.

Mass and the Presiding Celebrant

"No other single factor affects the liturgy as much as the attitude, style and bearing of the celebrant" – USA Bishops' Committee on the Liturgy.[1]

If the faithful are to be actively engaged in and enriched by the rite of Mass something more than valid, lawful and devout celebration on the part of the priest will be required.

Priests of pre-conciliar vintage were trained in the seminary to say Mass validly, lawfully and devoutly. Today something more is required *(SC 11)*. For one thing we speak of the priest as *presiding* at Mass rather than *saying* or even *celebrating* Mass. (Each member of the assembled people can be called a 'celebrant' since the entire assembly celebrates). And presiding involves trying to make text and ritual come alive in such a way that Mass will truly become for the people an experience of God.

A further requirement on the part of the presiding celebrant is a thorough understanding and grasp of the norms contained in the *General Instruction of the Roman Missal.* Such is essential if he is to be able to shape the celebration according to the needs of each particular congregation and occasion. And it is the starting point for any kind of creativity in the eucharistic liturgy.

With this in mind, and in the hope that they will open a window on the spirit as well as the letter of the Mass of the Roman Rite, the following notes are offered. For the sake of completeness and at the risk of a slight repetitiveness some points already made will of necessity have to be brought together again at this stage.

Mass as envisaged in the Roman Rite falls into four parts:

Introductory Rites
Liturgy of the Word

1. *Music in Catholic Worship,* National Conference of Catholic Bishops, 1983, page 18.

Liturgy of the Eucharist
Concluding Rite

1. Introductory Rites

From beginning of Mass to Opening Prayer, inclusive. (As he approaches each part of the Mass, and each element within each part, the priest should hold in his thoughts the following question: what is happening, and what precisely is my role at this point, vis-à-vis the people?).

Here at the beginning of Mass the challenge is to try to bond the people into a unified commuity, and to dispose them for the celebration *(cf IGMR 24)*. This is the moment of "gathering" when the people become aware of themselves as the bonded "People of God", assembled in a spirit of festive joy around their risen Lord. The aim of the Introductory Rites is to help bring about such an awareness. The physical environment, the artistic and architectural setting, the music, the incense, the ceremonial, the way the people relate to one another in a warm human manner, and, above all, the attitude and bearing of the priest – all combine to bring about the kind of atmosphere in which people will more easily centre upon the celebration of the sacred mysteries.

Entrance procession. Occasionally, eg, at the great festivals or even at the principal Mass each Sunday, a more solemn form of entrance might be used. The carrying of cross, incense and lighted candles adds such a note of solemnity. A reader may carry the book of the Gospels. The movement of the procession through the assembly helps to secure the people's attention: in spirit they move with priest and ministers into the presence of the Lord.

Opening song. This has a unifying effect. It helps create an atmosphere of festivity, and introduces the people to the mystery of the feast or season being celebrated. One could describe it as a 'gathering' song.

Choir, cantor and congregation. Music and song help create an atmosphere of festivity, solemnity and joy. Singing liberates people from their individualism, brings about an awareness that they are indeed a "people", the "People of God", and gives deeper meaning to their words. Singing is the sign of the heart's joy *(IGMR 19):* we sing because we have something to sing about.

The Church envisages "the whole body of the faithful" singing at

Mass *(SC 114)*. The choir's role is to lead and support the congregation, not to take over from them; the choir's secondary role is to sing the parts proper to them.

A good cantor or lead-singer (and it ought to be possible to discover and form one or two such people in every church) can give spirit to the people's singing. Clarity of words, too, is more readily achieved with a single cantor than with a group.

Altar. Table of banquet, altar of sacrifice – the use of both expressions reminds us that the Mass is "at one and the same time and inseparably a banquet and a sacrifice . . ." *(EM 3);* it is through and by means of the banquet that the sacrifice is made present in our midst, so that we can be personally involved in offering it. Traditionally the altar/table is reserved for the two breads, the bread of the word (Gospel book) and the bread of the eucharist (Blessed Sacrament). It should be free therefore of unnecessary objects like charts, altar cruets, bookstands. It is not prepared (see below) until the Preparation of the Gifts.

Veneration of Altar. The priest greets the altar not just to fulfil a rubrical requirement, but out of reverence for its sacredness, a reverence which will be reflected in his bearing and pace. Reverence is expressed through the profound bow, the kiss, the incensation. As the priest greets the altar the people too will be inspired to bow and bend low in their hearts *(cf Ps 95:6)*. The incensation of the altar, a 900 year old tradition, is a reminder of the attitude of prayer and awe which should characterise the worshippers.

The Chair. It is from the chair, and not from ambo or altar, that the priest greets the people. The chair has a theological significance. It marks the place of presidency from which the priest presides *in persona Christi,* in the person of Christ. The Church teaches that the presence of Christ in the priest is a *real* presence *(EM 9)* in that it is Christ who reaches out to people through the words, the gestures and the whole humanity of the priest. In that sense we can consider the chair as the 'chair of Christ'. The priest remains at the chair until he moves to the ambo to proclaim the word.

The Sign of the Cross. The sign of the cross bonds us to God and to one another. It should be made purposefully, drawing the people into an attitude of dialogue and response.

Greeting. Routine can dull the priest's awareness of what he is doing here. The purpose of the greeting is to make the people aware of the presence of the risen Lord. Eye contact is important: the priest ought to relate to the people, not to the book. Hands reach out towards them in a gesture of greeting, welcome and embrace.

Introductory words. A short, carefully prepared introduction can create an effective rapport between priest and people, setting the scene, and focussing their attention on what they are about. Clichéd introductions, such as those beginning with the words "In today's readings" should be avoided. So should 'sermonitis', the tendency towards over-talk at Mass.

Penitential Rite. Mass is not a gathering of the perfect. Standing before God on the threshold of our worship we are conscious of our failings, our brokenness, and our need for reconciliation with God and with one another. It is interesting to recall that the Greek *Kyrie eleison* has praise overtones, as well as being a cry for mercy: we praise God because he is merciful. Emphasis ought to be on the Lord (and his forgiveness) rather than on ourselves (and the details of how we may have failed). For this reason the invocations in the third form of the penitential rite are addressed to the Second Person of the Trinity: "*You* were sent to heal the contrite." That is the model the priest should follow if he is composing his own invocations, and not the self-centred wording one sometimes hears such as "For the times *I* failed . . ."

Gloria. The Gloria belongs to the people. For this reason it may be better for a cantor to intone it, as a representative of the people. Originally the Gloria was an Easter morning hymn. Gradually it found its way into the Roman Mass. It reflects the joyful, festive character of the Christian celebration of the Lord's day, and is one of the most beautiful and most popular of ancient Christian hymns.

Opening Prayer. The priest's task here is not simply to pray a formulary, but to actually facilitate the people's praying. An occasional reminder to the people that we are going to pause for a few moments of silence during which we make our petitions to God can be highly effective. The manner too in which the priest says "Let us pray" should help to ease the people into a mood of deeply interior prayer in which they implore God for their own *personal* needs (later in the prayer of the faithful they will pray for *universal* needs). Special attention should be paid to the concluding doxology, which is trinitarian: in the strength of the Spirit we go to the Father through Christ who is our Way.

2. Liturgy of the Word

From the first reading to prayer of the faithful, inclusive. In the liturgy of the word Christ himself speaks to the assembled people. They in turn respond through their reverent listening, their song and their prayer. At the same time the Spirit is at work in them, empowering them to live out their faith daily, and to witness to Christ before the world.

The liturgy of the word is not merely didactic. Nor is it merely preparatory. Its purpose is not simply to instruct, or to prepare the congregation for the sacrifice. It is in itself a celebration in praise of God, a proclamation of his wonders. What is proclaimed in the word is actualised in the eucharist. The two, word and eucharist, form a single act of worship. That is why they should not take place separately or in different places.

From the two tables, therefore, the faithful are nourished: from the table of the word and the table of the eucharist. The Church has always honoured the word and the eucharistic mystery with the same reverence, although not with the same worship. That is why a period of silence is recommended in the celebration of the word, to allow us to savour the bread of the word, just as later on at Mass we savour the bread of the eucharist by taking it to heart, pondering it, responding to it.

The elements which comprise the liturgy of the word are: Scripture readings, chants, homily, silence, Creed, prayer of the faithful.

Sunday Mass has three readings: from the Old Testament, usually; from an Apostle, and from the Gospels. The Gospel is semi-continuous on Sundays in ordinary time. The first reading is chosen on the basis of some link with the Gospel. But the second, like the Gospel, is semi-continuous. During Advent, Lent and Easter the three readings are harmonised.

Introducing the readings. A brief introduction to the readings, or to each one separately, can prepare the people to listen attentively and take to heart their meaning. The playing of reflective music, eg, on organ, flute or guitar as the reader walks to the ambo can help create a mood of expectation: "When peaceful silence lay over all, and night had run half her swift course, your all-powerful word leaped down, Lord, leaped down from heaven." *(Ws 18:14-15)*[2]

2. Entrance antiphon, Sunday after Christmas.

The Reader. The reader should be a lay person. "The liturgical assembly truly requires readers, even those not instituted" *(DVD 52)*. The Church directs that each person in the assembly should carry out that part, and only that part, which belongs to him or her *(IGMR 58)*. The priest therefore should not act as reader.

The reader at the ambo is God's mouthpiece. The attitude and bearing of the reader should reflect an understanding of and appreciation of what is being read. The Church requires that readers be "competent and carefully prepared for their task" *(IGMR 66)*. In addition to their technical training, to ensure that the reading will be clear and intelligent, a spiritual preparation is necessary: this requires that readers have a clear grasp of and conviction about the central message of the passage in question, and a concern to share that conviction with the congregation. That is why there is need for prayerful study of and reflection on the passage before proclaiming it at Mass.

The Ambo. The ambo is reserved for the readings, the responsorial psalm, and the Easter *Exultet.* It may be used also for the homily and the intercessions at the prayer of the faithful. It is better for the cantor and the director of the singing not to use it. Nor should it be used for announcements. It is the place for the proclamation of the word, and in its very design it should reflect the dignity of the word.

Gospel Book and Lectionary. In the Church's tradition the books which contain the sacred scriptures have always been the object of care and veneration. They enshrine the sacred texts through which God speaks to his people. Current legislation requires that "the books, as symbols of the supernatural in the liturgical celebration, be of high quality, tastefully, and even beautifully, produced" *(DVD 35)*. Illuminations, bindings and book-shrines show that they are precious objects – like the Book of Kells, for example, one of the most beautiful books ever written. In liturgical tradition the Gospel book is venerated with a kiss and with incensation.

The Old Testament Readings. The entire bible speaks of Christ, the Old Testament as well as the New. The entire bible was written, as St Paul reminds us, "for our instruction". To understand Christ, therefore, we must turn also to the Old Testament. The New lies hidden in the Old; the Old comes fully to light in the New.[3]

The Reponsorial Psalm. The psalm is an integral part of the word,

3. In this context I recall the answer of the child who said that the Old Testament is "the story of Jesus before he was born".

and should not be replaced by a non-scriptural song. Through the psalm the people express their response to God's word, and at the same time savour and ponder that word. As a rule the psalm should be sung. The challenge to the person singing it, the psalmist, is to hold the faithful in an attitude of prayerful pondering of the word, and to articulate in his or her singing "the song in the heart, the prayer in the soul". The psalmist sings the verses, and the people the responses. Alternatively, the psalm may be sung by the psalmist alone, or the congregation together.

It seems necessary to remind psalmists, or the person reading the psalm, to avoid saying "response" after each verse – a practice which gives an infantile and hollow ring to the celebration. For purposes of cueing in the people it is sufficient that the reader read intelligently, with suitable changing of pace, emphasis and tone at the end of each verse. Moreover, if it is felt that the response given in the lectionary for a particular Mass is too difficult one should select a suitable alternative.

The Alleluia or verse before the Gospel. This should be sung; in it the people welcome and salute the Lord who is about to address them. A procession with incense and candles and the carrying of a beautiful Gospel book can help emphasise the proclamation of the Gospel as the highpoint of the Liturgy of the Word. The Gospel is read by a deacon or by a second priest if Mass is concelebrated; otherwise by the presiding priest.

The Homily. The homily "sets forth the mysteries of faith and the standards of Christian life on the basis of the sacred text" *(DVD 24).* God speaks to the faithful in the readings. The homilist's task is to help the people hear and take that message to heart. The homily should lead the people also to celebrate the eucharist wholeheartedly so that they may hold fast in their lives to what they have heard in the scriptures.

Since the homily is part of the liturgy itself the sign of the cross is not to be made after the homily.

Silence. The liturgy of the word is a time for savouring the bread of the word, for pausing like Mary to ponder in the heart. "Any kind of haste is to be totally avoided, because it impedes recollection. Dialogue between God and his people, with the help of the holy Spirit, requires short periods of silence, adjusted to the assembly, during which the heart opens to the word of God and a prayerful response takes shape" *(DVD 128)*. "These are very fruitful silences" writes Sister Maria Boulding. "They gather up the silences of our individual lives, of our days, of our personal prayer."[4]

The Creed. Ever since the eleventh century the Creed has been said at Sunday Mass in the Roman Rite. In the Creed we respond and give assent to the Word of God which we have heard in the scriptures and in the homily. The Creed is also a time to profess our belief in the mysteries of our faith which are at the heart of our Mass and our life.

As an alternative the Apostles' Creed may be used at Mass with the required permission.[5]

Prayer of the Faithful. Through baptism Christians become members of a royal priesthood with the task, as St Paul urges, of offering "petitions, prayers and intercessions for all" *(1 Tm 2:1)*. Their privileged moment for exercising this sharing in Christ's priestly intercession is at the Prayer of the Faithful, when they join Christ in praying for the church and the world. Already around the year 150 St Justin tells how the faithful, following the homily, would stand and offer intense prayers for themselves and for all people. Today as a rule our petitions have to do with the needs of the Church, the needs of civil authorities, the salvation of the world, the suffering and the local community.

The curious practice of adding a Hail Mary to the Prayer of the Faithful is scarcely to be recommended. According to a letter of the Sacred Congregation for Divine Worship in 1973 the use of such prayers as the Hail Mary, the Hail Holy Queen, the Regina Coeli and the Memorare "are not in harmony with the structure of the Prayer of the Faithful". Any reference to Mary should be in a manner which harmonises with the rest of the Prayer of the Faithful as for example with the following petition: "For all who see their loved ones suffer, that God will give them courage like the courage of Mary at the foot of the cross."

The priest introduces the prayer. A deacon or one of the faithful announces the intentions. The people respond after each intercession, or pray silently. The priest concludes the prayer.

4. In *New Liturgy,* Autumn 1981.

5. That permission has been granted, for example, to Ireland. See *New Liturgy,* Spring 1986, page 5.

3. *Liturgy of the Eucharist*

This comprises:
(a) Preparation of the Gifts
(b) Eucharistic Prayer
(c) Communion Rite

(a) Preparation of the Gifts

This 'holy space' between liturgy of the word and the eucharistic prayer allows people to interiorise and prepare silently for the eucharistic prayer when they join Christ in praising the Father and offering the sacrifice. For this reason the priest says the prayers during the preparation of the gifts in silence. In comparison with the eucharistic prayer, which is the highpoint of the celebration, the preparation of the gifts is simple, and ought not to be so built up (eg, through over-elaborate processions) as to overshadow the great eucharistic prayer. For this and other reasons the carrying of gifts and symbolic objects, eg, school books, and tools should be avoided; only bread, wine and gifts for the Church or the poor may be carried in the procession.

Preparation of the Altar. The altar should be kept bare so that it can be dressed at this point – although the altar cloth and candles may be on it from the beginning. Altar cloth (unless it is already on the altar), corporal, purificator and missal are now placed in position. The missal can be placed directly in front of the priest instead of to one side.

The Collection. In practice, the collection sometimes appears as an unwelcome intrusion into the Mass. In fact it can be of powerful symbolic value. It is a practice which goes back to the very beginnings of Christianity. It reminds us that going to Mass puts on us the obligation to give, to share, to work for social justice in the world. Our donation becomes a sign of our willingness as Christians to help our brothers and sisters in need.

The collection needs to be handled efficiently, and need only take a minute or two. The priest might sit and wait meantime, so that the collection will not appear to intrude, but rather to sensitise people with regard to their duties to those in want.

Procession. The involvement of the people in the procession with the gifts underlines the active role which they as baptised Christians have in the offering of the Mass. The procession can convey the idea also of the people's entering into the sacrifice. The bread and wine are symbols of God's gifts of food and life, and are destined to become the bread of life and spiritual drink. If the procession is to 'speak', it should be planned with care; the gifts should be carried in a ritualised or stylised manner, reverently and lovingly.

Bread and Wine. The bread should look like bread, and be large enough to be broken and shared by at least some of the congregation. As far as possible the communicants should receive from bread consecrated at the Mass they are attending. When their number cannot be estimated beforehand, enough bread should be consecrated for distribution among part of the congregation at least.

Because of the symbolism of unity in the "one bread and one cup" it is desirable to use a single paten, dish or ciborium; and a single chalice if communion is to be distributed under both kinds; additional flagons may be used if necessary, and the precious blood transferred to communion cups at the fraction.

Prayers of the Priest. The priest, as a norm, is silent during the preparation of the gifts, saying the various prayers *secreto.* If there is no singing the priest may say aloud the blessing prayers over the bread and wine, and these alone. The reasoning behind this arrangement in the Roman rite is that the prayers at this point are by their very nature the private prayers of the priest "with the purpose of helping him to exercise his ministry with attention and devotion" *(IGMR 13).* The 'holy silence' which results allows the faithful to prepare spiritually for the sacrifice. Quiet, meditative music can facilitate their prayer.

Priest's Gestures. While he says the blessing prayers the priest holds the paten and later the chalice slightly raised. This is a gesture not of offering (the offering comes during eucharistic prayer), but of designation and acknowledgement.

Incensation is permitted at this point. The cloud of incense is evocative of the cloud through which the glory of the Lord appeared to the Israelites in the desert. Incense helps to create that attitude of reverence with ought to characterise the celebration of the sacred mysteries. The faithful too are incensed: through baptism they are holy and consecrated; their bodies are the temples of the Spirit. The incensation should be handled therefore in an expressive, evocative way.

"Pray, my brothers and sisters . . ." The priest should wait until the people have finished their response before proceeding. All accessories, jug, cruets, finger bowl, towel, should be removed from the altar.

(b) Eucharistic Prayer

The dialogue "The Lord be with you . . . Lift up your hearts . . ." brings us to the highpoint of the celebration, the eucharistic prayer. This prayer is a great proclamation of praise and thanksgiving to God. In the eucharistic prayer the Church in obedience to our Lord's command "Do this in memory of me" does what Jesus did at the last Supper – gives thanks and praise to the Father. The priest is the people's spokesman; he alone proclaims the prayer, doing so on behalf of and in the name of the people. As he prays aloud they pray in silence, pondering the words, interiorising them, taking them to heart. Apart from the acclamations – the Holy, Holy, the memorial acclamation and the great Amen the priest's voice alone is heard; this holds also for the doxology; "Through him, with him."

During the eucharistic prayer the faithful join Christ in thanking and praising the Father, and in offering the sacrifice. "Thanking and praising the Father" and "offering the sacrifice" are basic Christian acts of worship. In the eucharistic prayer the people's thanks is 'christified', transformed, offered to the Father through Christ, with Christ and in Christ. In offering the spotless victim the faithful learn to offer themselves too, pledging themselves to the living out of the Christian way of life, even if this should mean for them a cross.

During the eucharistic prayer the bread and wine, through the power of the Spirit, become the body and blood of Christ, so that his sacrifice, offered once for all on the cross, becomes present in our midst. In that way the faithful can be personally involved in the sacrifice, uniting themselves with Christ in his offering, and communing in his body and blood.

The following points relating to the eucharistic prayer should be kept in mind:

(i) The wording of the eucharistic prayer is the Church's expression of what she believes and wishes to express about the eucharist. The wording, therefore, enshrines eucharistic doctrine and ought not to be tampered with.

(ii) The eucharistic prayer is a unit, not therefore to be broken. This calls for a single posture throughout the prayer. The point is scarcely appreciated by people who sit passively during the preface, then adopt a posture of reverent kneeling at the Holy, Holy. The preface is not an introduction, but part of the eucharistic prayer itself (the word itself, 'preface' is from *prae fari* – to speak or cry out in praise of someone). Already in the preface we are into the *inner sanctum* of the eucharist.

(iii) The Church has a variety of eucharistic prayers: four in the missal, together with five for Masses with Children and Masses of Reconciliation. All prayers should be used from time to time, depending on the circumstances. By hearing the different prayers at different times the faithful will become more familiar with the thoughts enshrined in them and will gain deeper access into an understanding of the eucharistic mystery, and deeper appreciation of its riches.

(iv) The spirit of the eucharistic prayer as grateful acknowledgement of the works of God *(cf IGMR 54)* is expressed more effectively, and the people's attention more firmly secured, when priest and people sing the parts proper to them: in the case of the priest the preface, doxology and even on occasion the entire prayer; in the case of the people the Holy, Holy, the memorial acclamation, and the great Amen.

(v) The missal directs that the people adopt a standing posture during the eucharistic prayer, although bishops may decide on other postures for their own people.[6] Standing is the traditional posture for Christian prayer. It expresses the liberty of the Christian, who has been lifted up from slavery. It shows too that the people, like the priest, are actively involved in the offering of the Mass.[7]

At the end of the eucharistic prayer the people sing the acclamation with which they confirm and conclude the praise offered to God by the priest, the 'great Amen'. This is a

6. ie, the Bishops' Conference. See *IGMR 21.*

7. See chapter *Externals,* above.

glorious and majestic moment, and it calls for song. Merely to say the Amen is to do less than justice to its rich implications. In that little word is encapsuled the gratitude which lies in people's hearts, their sorrow for sin, their sense of dependence on God. The great Amen is their 'yes' to God, their 'yes' to Christianity, their 'yes' to following the Christian way, even if this is to mean a cross.

(vi) The following might be noted regarding the priest's words during the eucharistic prayer. First, with reference to his tone of voice: he should avoid both a dry and monotonous tone on the one hand, and a tone which is too subjective and emotional on the other. As he leads the people into the heart of the Mass with the words "Lift up your hearts" he should keep in mind that in the eucharist heaven comes down on earth, and mortals and heavenly powers join with one voice in the offering of the eternal liturgy. The priest may give a short word of introduction before the preface. Finally, at the Holy, Holy, he would be advised to wait until the acclamation is over before turning the pages of the missal.

(vii) Special attention ought to be paid to the gestures during the eucharistic prayer, as follows. Epiclesis: the out-stretched hands of the priest suggest the coming down of the Spirit to sanctify the gifts. Elevation of host and chalice: this is a gesture of showing, not of offering. Doxology, "Through him, with him, in him . . .": the priest's gesture here is a large gesture of praise and offering. From what has been said already under 'Bread and wine' it should be obvious that it is preferable to hold up only the one paten and the one chalice at the doxology during a concelebrated Mass.

(viii) The acclamation after the words of institution is a proclamation of the faithful's belief in the paschal mystery, that is the death, resurrection, glorification and final coming of Christ. It includes, but is much more than, an expression of belief in the real presence. Hence a chant such as "Come let us adore him" which is known to have been heard at Christmas Masses, is inadequate and ought not to be used.

(c) Communion Rite

Two complementary and inseparable aspects of the Mass are the banquet aspect and the sacrifice aspect. It is through the banquet that the sacrifice is made present in our midst. Communicating in the banquet is the more perfect form of offering the sacrifice: "Mass is at one and the same time and inseparably a sacrifice in which the sacrifice of the cross is perpetuated; a memorial of the death and resurrection of the Lord . . . and a sacred banquet in which, through the communion of the body and blood of the Lord, the people of God share the benefits of the paschal sacrifice, renew the new covenant which God has made with humankind once and for all through the blood of Christ, and in faith and hope foreshadow and anticipate the eschatological banquet in the kingdom of the Father, proclaiming the Lord's death until he comes" *(EM 3)*. At Communion time above all we think of our Lord beckoning us and welcoming us, sinners though we are, to the intimacy of his table.

The altar should be so designed and appointed that the faithful can easily recognise it as the table of the sacred banquet as well as the altar of sacrifice.

The Our Father. This prayer introduces the final part of the liturgy of the eucharist, the Communion rite. For 1600 years the Lord's Prayer has been said at Mass. Its references to our daily bread and to forgiveness, God's forgiveness of us and our forgiveness of one another, make it the perfect communal preparation for Communion. Communion itself presupposes unity and mutual peace among believers. And so we beg God for these gifts, and offer one another a sign and pledge of our peace and forgiveness.

The Our Father of course belongs to the whole congregation, and should not be taken over by the choir to the exclusion of the general body of the faithful.

Sign of peace. From the foregoing it should be clear that the sign of peace is not in the order of a greeting, welcome or hello; it is a sincere prayer for and pledge to live a life of reconciliation and love.

Lamb of God. This prayer or chant accompanies the breaking of the bread, and may be repeated as often as is necessary whenever the breaking of the bread is prolonged as, eg, in a concelebrated Mass, or in a Mass where the kind of large host envisioned in the missal is used. This is also the time, as we have already noted, for transferring consecrated wine, when necessary, into communion cups.

Fraction. The 'breaking of the bread' is related to the unity of the Church. "Though we are many", says St Paul, "we are all one body, because we all share in the one loaf." Those who share in the one bread and cup themselves become one in Christ. The author of the *Didaché,* writing in the first century, saw a powerful symbol of unity in the bread "formed from many grains gathered from many hills". Because of this symbolism the bread should be large enough to be broken and shared by at least some of the faithful. By raising the bread high and breaking it in a deliberate and clearly visible manner the priest can facilitate and heighten the faithful's awareness of the symbolism.

"Lord Jesus Christ, Son of the living God . . ." This prayer, like the prayers during the preparation of the gifts, is a private prayer of the priest, to be said therefore in silence.

"This is the Lamb of God . . ." As the faithful respond to the priest's invitation they gaze with faith and love on the eucharistic bread. In almost every rite there is a formal invitation to Communion. In the Byzantine rite, for instance, one hears the words: "Holy things for the holy . . . with awe, with faith and with love draw near" to the sacred banquet.

Communion procession. The Roman rite envisages a ritual procession. In practice the procession usually takes the form of a functional, physical movement of the people towards the point of distribution. One appreciates the effect of a procession of a united, joy-filled people, bonded together in the Lord, singing a single song, and united in a fellowship of a common faith, a common hope, a common love.

Communion. As each one approaches, the minister holds the host before the communicant's gaze saying "The Body of Christ," speaking the words in such a way as to elicit a heartfelt "Amen", and placing the host with reverence, feeling and love on the hand or tongue. The response 'Amen' is a response of faith in the real presence, a response of welcome, a response of commitment to the Lord and to the Christian way of life. In this it is an echo at deeply personal level of the great Amen of the eucharistic prayer.

"The person who eats my flesh and drinks my blood is united to me and I am united to that person." Holy Communion means intimacy, total intimacy, with Jesus-Eucharist. One can say about our Lord at this moment, in the words of the Song of Songs: "My beloved is mine, and I am his" *(Sg 2:16).* Through our shared intimacy with Jesus-Eucharist we are united also to one another in a communion which we must try to live out each day in mutual love and forgiveness and concern. Communion too means communion in Jesus' sacrifice. It means commitment to a way of life which will entail suffering, the suffering of the cross.

Sometimes one notices communicants making the sign of the cross on receiving communion. It is a beautiful and laudable practice: as the Lord comes to us we identify ourselves with the Christian mark with which we were signed at baptism, the first sacrament by which we were introduced into the mystery of Christ's sacrifice. It reminds us too that communion means *communing* in Jesus' sacrifice, communing in his commitment to the ultimate degree to the will of the Father.

Communion song. This song is intended to accompany the procession, a procession which, as we pointed out earlier, is of a joy-filled people, bonded together in the Lord, and singing together a single song as they move towards his table. It is to be distinguished from the hymn of praise or psalm which may be sung when all are seated after communion.

Communion silence. When communion is over the faithful may be invited to pray and ponder in silence. These are golden moments of intimate union with the Lord, moments for praying in the heart, for interiorising, for personalising our praise and thanks and petition. They are moments too of wonderment and adoration and awareness of the Lord. A few words from the priest can be useful in stimulating the people's prayer, but the priest should avoid the excess of words which leaves the faithful with no space to commune interiorly.

In certain circumstances the people may receive from the chalice. This brings out more clearly the banquet aspect of the eucharist. Sinners though we are, God beckons us in a gesture of divine intimacy and love to share at his table. The precious blood reminds us too of the new Covenant, sealed in the blood of Christ, to which we as Christians are pledged.

The chalice should be given over completely into the hands of the communicant. To tilt the chalice towards the communicant while still holding on to it is to risk spilling the precious blood.

The sacred vessels can be left over, if the priest so wishes, and cleansed after Mass – in which case they may be placed on the altar or on a side table.

4. Concluding Rite

Following the Prayer after Communion.

Announcements. Any announcements to be made may be made at this point, and not, as one sometimes finds, before the Prayer after Communion – in which case they become an intrusion into what is an especially sacred moment.

Dismissal. Before bringing the celebration to a close the priest may say a final word to the people. With the 'dismissal' we have come to the moment of mission, in which the people, with God's blessing on them, are sent out to celebrate the liturgy of the world. Their task now is to carry the Christian message to the world, to make their lives a living sacrifice, to preach the Gospel by the way they live, and to go on breaking bread with their brothers and sisters in need.